La Cucina

A Sicilian Ame

Carmela Cusumano
July 31, 1922–November 19, 2015

For my husband, Charlie, a man of good taste,

hearty appetite, and other rare distinctions

Centanni Publications
Slow-cooked words for hungry minds
www.centannipublications.com

San Francisco, California

La Cucina di Carmela
Copyright © 2008, 2015, 2018, Estate of Carmela Cusumano
Printed in the United States of America
Centanni Publications, San Francisco, California

SECOND EDITION

ISBN-13: 978-0997049893
ISBN-10: 0997049898

Book cover & interior design, cover photo, and author photo:
Valentina Dante
Interior photos: Property of Cusumano estate

Requests for permission to reprint material:
Centanni Publications
ocaramia2000@gmail.com
(415) 425-6515
www.centannipublications.com

Centanni Publications
Slow-cooked words for hungry minds
www.centannipublications.com
San Francisco, California

Dear Friends and Fans of Carmela,

Welcome to an expanded second edition of **La Cucina di Carmela**. We have added more than two dozen new recipes, a few more stories and photos of Carmela, Charles, and the family. We hope you will enjoy all the new and the old recipes and our stories. We love to hear from you if you have any questions, comments, or even corrections—see contact info on page 2. Buon Appetito, Tutti!

Foreword from Carmela's ten children (first edition):
Welcome to La Cucina di Carmela!

Our mother Carmela Cusumano passed away peacefully on November 19, 2015. She was 93. In her mid-80s, our mother had assembled this cookbook, published it spiral-bound, and shared it with family and friends.

In that first edition, 2008, she wrote:

"For many years, my children would call me and ask how to cook a certain recipe they remembered—that Broccoli Soup or Pizza the way we ate it on Fridays when meat was forbidden. So for many years I've wanted to collect these recipes in one place. As time went on, I also added new recipes from good friends who enjoyed the simple pleasures of cooking and eating. You'll find recipes as humble as Pasta and Peas and as fancy as Beef Wellington. As some guy, I think he was French, said: *To eat is a necessity, to eat well is an art.* That's why I am so excited to finally present these recipes, old and new ones, to my ten children, their spouses and partners, my twenty-four grandchildren, my fifteen great-grandchildren, plus, at this writing, the seven great-grand-kids on the way (in the oven, so to speak) and to my many good friends. As we Sicilians say, *a tavola, mangiamo. Buon appetito!*"

First let us note that since 2008, the number of Mom's great-grandchildren has increased significantly. We won't set that number in ink as it is always changing, almost annually.

—

Carmela, born a Catalano, was the daughter of Sicilian immigrants. She was born in Peterstown, an Italian enclave in Elizabeth, New Jersey, also known as the Berg, that still thrives. She met our father, Charles (Calogero) Anthony, also born in Peterstown to Sicilian parents, when she was 16. They married in July, 1941, just before her 19th birthday. Their oldest child, James Anthony, would be born while Dad was at war in the Pacific Theater. Dad returned when his son was one-and-a-half and our parents proceeded to conceive a child, six girls and four boys, about every other year until 1960 when the last child, Donna Gina, was born.

Mom loved being a dutiful wife and mother. She bore up through our years of growing up under many stresses and challenges of a big family. She never seemed to tire of having to feed a brood. She cooked to nourish us. She cooked to give us pleasure. She had taken home economics in Battin High School (she was the first in her family to make it past fifth grade). As you will note she loved baked goods, not just Italian, but all types.

Mom was a typical old-world Sicilian housewife, deferring to her husband, usually without complaint. She was mostly content to abide by his old-fashioned ways. Dad revered food in that almost sacred way that Italians are famous for. He demanded that we eat bread at every meal to better fill our bellies. He demanded we clean our plates and we did. So did he. He made Mom serve us first, him last.

He was not above cooking or butting in and telling Mom how to embellish a dish. Sometimes she had to shoo him away. We have added to Mom's book Dad's famous meatloaf recipe, which changed depending on the amount and type of ingredients in the refrigerator. Dad could be very creative with leftovers (we never threw food out). In later years when we fled the nest, Dad loved making their homemade sausage from scratch with Mom. And bread and ravioli and other types of pasta. He even joined in her cookie making. He loved especially making Mom's Fig Cookies (called *cucidati,* which

In Sicilian sounds like *widgie-dah* to our American ears because Sicilian dialect often drops syllables).

Through the years of having twelve mouths to feed on a postal worker's paycheck, the food was simple and good, a mix of basic Sicilian dishes as well as American fare. We knew our food was different from what our friends ate *and* we knew it was exceptional because our friends loved to be invited to eat with us. Especially when it was macaroni (we didn't call it pasta back then) or pizza pie.

After Mom died, we decided to re-publish her cookbook to share with anyone who loves food or cooking. There are many simple dishes here. There are a few fancy dishes, like beef wellington, which Mom collected after we were grown and gone and she could afford the time and money for such dishes.

Food is love. Food holds deep recall. Our eating culture has become wonderfully complex, yet at times too *outré,* over the top with involved, difficult, time-consuming steps. However, some of the recipes here are steeped in a different sort of richness and complexity, that of the memory of what nurtured our bodies and souls, our early tender years of growing up, things as simple as garlicky greens.

Mom was a busy full-time housewife and mother through the 1950s and '60s, so some of her recipes reflect those times. She was not above using some canned or packaged ingredients (which some of us in later years pooh-poohed). If you are old enough to recall those years, and grew up New Jersey, you might recall that the produce available to us was much more limited than what we have today. So we ate canned peas and legumes, canned French-cut string beans, canned Le Sueur peas, frozen spinach.

However, our grandparents had a garden and they grew Italian vegetables and the dark greens that are highly revered today—Swiss chard, dandelions, broccoli rabe (*rapini*)—but that were nowhere to be found in stores back then. And there was an Italian market in Peterstown, Elizabeth, that carried many of the foodstuffs that our immi-grant relatives recalled from the old country.

—
5

Although most of us consider that butter has no substitute, Mom calls for margarine *or* butter in her recipes. The fat we consumed most as kids naturally was olive oil. Big gallon tins of Gemma or Progresso brands olive oil. We never counted calories. If anything we counted mouthfuls of nourishment and pleasure.

A word on the recipe directions: Mom wrote many of these recipes as if she were talking directly to the cook. We decided to keep this "folksy" aspect, that is our Mother's own wording as much as possible. We did go through her recipes and correct any confusion or make little helpful notes. (All oven temperatures are Fahrenheit.) Most of her recipes are pretty simple and require only a basic knowledge of cooking skills. However, if you find one that is so confusing or so unclear you need guidance, contact Carmela's daughter, Camille, by email at: **ocaramia2000@gmail.com.** You will note a lot of baked goods, one of Mom's favorite pastimes. Finally, no surprise, many recipes serve a crowd. *Buon appetito!*

—Carmela's Ten Children (James Anthony, Maria Theresa, Charles Anthony, Salvatore Joseph, Camille Jeanne, Grace Cecele, Thomas Edward, Lisa Ann, Tina Marie, Donna Gina), December 2015

Carmela is seated at table in the striped blouse. Photo is circa mid-1960s. Eight of the ten kids are present. Only Jim and Sal are missing—probably, we concluded, off doing mad-scientist work in the cellar. Dad likely took the photo. Also present are Grandma Cusumano (front right), Uncle Tony (behind Grandma), Aunts Mary and Agnes, to left of Tony, and cousins Bernice, Maryanne, Gregory. And John Hennessy, Terry's then-husband. Note, this is our kitchen on Price Street, Rahway, NJ, about 100 square feet, where we ate our meals and often gathered with company no matter how many dropped by (the door was always open, never locked).

TABLE OF CONTENTS

Carmela as a blushing bride, 1941

Eggplant Salad *(Capunatina)*

This is a nice appetizer and also good with cold cuts or as a topping for pasta

Yield: 10 to 12 Servings as appetizer, 6 to 8 as entrée with pasta

2 Large Eggplants
1/2 Cup Olive Oil
2 Large Onions, Chopped
4 Stalks Celery, Chopped
1 Large Can Crushed Tomatoes
4 Tablespoons Fresh Basil or 1 Teaspoon Dried Basil
1 Teaspoon Salt
1 Teaspoon Crushed Red Pepper
1/4 Cup Capers
1 Cup Green Olives, Chopped
2 Tablespoons Sugar
1/4 Cup Wine Vinegar, or To Taste

Peel eggplant and cut in cubes about 1-inch. Put in colander and salt lightly and let stand for 1 hour to let bitter juices drain. Rinse eggplant and squeeze well. Pour oil in large fry pan, add eggplant, onions, celery, tomatoes, basil, salt, pepper, capers, olives, sugar, and vinegar. Simmer about 20 to 30 minutes. Adjust seasoning to taste. This can be put in sterile pint jars or refrigerate and serve as an appetizer, chilled or room temperature.

Folk Wisdom & Facts

Sicilians and most other Italians have opinions that come across as articles of faith. Mom and Dad preferred only what they called red or purple garlic. We cannot tell you why, but most likely it is milder than the whiter version. They preferred flatleaf or Italian parsley to the crinkly one, which is sharper and more bitter. Those are easily tested opinions and affirmed or negated as you please. The salt tossed in spilled olive oil to keep away bad luck, well, we love the ritual of it. Not one of us can sit still and do nothing if we see a loaf of bread resting upside down. This must never happen, a veritable sacrilege. All of our forebears had a fit if bread was turned top down. With apologies to the gluten-intolerant, bread (or more likely wheat) is part of holy trinity that includes the olive and the grape. The Sicilian journal, *Arba Sicula,* published an explanation years ago. It appears that long ago, somewhere in Sicily an executioner used to pass by a baker's window. In that olden time, when the baker forgot to save bread for the executioner, the baker's wife felt so sorry. From then on, she would turn one bread upside down for him to pick up each evening when he returned from the gallows. It sounds like a well-traveled superstition. However, we also think that there might well be something to the fact that Sicily was long ago bread basket to the Romans (who also didn't hesitate to shear off the islands virgin forests). So, please, keep your loaf of bread right-side up in our presence.

Boy and Girl Eggplants

We love assigning sex to our vegetables. Gram and Gramps instinctively knew that the heavier seedy one (female) was more bitter than the less seedy male. They even knew how to study the eggplant's bottom for an inny (female) or an outy (male) . . . let's call it tush. Alas, the botanical truth denies us this folklore. But not completely. To be sure, the flowers of the eggplant have both male and female organs. The eggplant fruits from the female organ, naturally. Apparently, the dimple at the bottom of the eggplant can appear roundish or oval, that is more narrow. The round feminine ones do seem to have more seeds. As with many other fruits and vegetables, buying a good eggplant means looking for healthy shiny skin, preferably unblemished. The eggplant should feel solid and compact, not wooden and light (indicating age and dryness). As for the oval or round bottom, let us know what your experience shows. And for the record, we never called it eggplant. We called it *mullinjohn*, our Anglicized pronunciation of the Sicilian *mullingian'* (none of us is sure of the spelling), which in proper Italian would be *melanzana*.

Crab Claw Appetizer

Daddy and I used to go to a restaurant in Texas with your Uncle Pat and Aunt Liz that served this dish. Whenever we went there they made this special appetizer. Aunt Liz managed to get the recipe from them and she gave it to me.

Yield: 6 Servings

1 Tablespoon Olive Oil
2 Large Shallots, Minced
4 Cloves Garlic, Minced, or ½ Tsp. granulated garlic
1 Teaspoon Tomato Paste
1 Tablespoon All Purpose Flour
1 Bottle (8 oz.) Clam Juice
1/4 Cup White Wine
2 Tablespoons Chopped Parsley
1/4 Teaspoon Black Pepper
2 Tablespoons Sweet Butter
2 Tablespoons Chopped Basil
1 Pound Crab Claws
Italian Bread and Lemon Wedges

Heat oil in skillet. Add shallots and garlic. Sauté till tender, about 3 minutes. Add tomato paste and stir together and add flour, constantly stirring till flour is golden. Add clam juice, wine, parsley and black pepper. Stir and bring to boil. Lower heat and sauté a few minutes. Add butter. Cook till melted. Add basil and remove from heat. When ready to serve add crab claws and heat till hot. Serve immediately with Italian Bread and lemon wedges.

Reuben Roll Ups

I was at a friend's home and she served this appetizer and I thought it was very good.

Yield: 16 Servings as an appetizer

Filling:
1 Package 3-Ounce Smoked Sliced Corned Beef, Finely Chopped
1 Cup Shredded Swiss Cheese, about 4 ounces
1/2 Cup Sauerkraut, Chopped
2 or 3 Tablespoons Water
Pastry:
1 Cup Flour
1/4 Cup Shortening
3 Ounces Cream Cheese
1 Teaspoon Caraway Seeds
1/8 Teaspoon Salt
Dressing:
1/4 Cup (4 Tablespoons) Bottled Thousand Island Dressing

Filling: Mix corned beef, Swiss cheese, sauerkraut, and water and set aside.

Pastry: Mix pastry ingredients like any pie dough and divide into two portions. Roll each portion into an 11 X 9 inch rectangle sheet. Spread each portion with 2 tablespoons of the dressing. Spread each rectangle with half of the corned beef mixture. Fold in ends. Roll up beginning at the 11-inch (longer) side; pinch edges to seal. Place the rolls on ungreased sheet. Bake 450 degrees for 15 to 20 minutes. Cut each roll into 4 pieces.

Note from us kids: If you don't know what "like any pie dough" means: Blend the ingredients with a fork until the mixture looks like coarse cornmeal. Then use your hands lightly to form a ball of dough. If dough is too dry, you can add a little ice water to help it cohere into a ball.

I Remember Mama

Terry (oldest daughter): I realized after listening to my other siblings' memories of Mom, that as the second oldest of our family of ten children I had a different growing up experience of observing and joining our mother with her extraordinary talent for baking and cooking. My experience in the 1950s was helping her in the kitchen but mostly by watching and helping her with taking care of the babies that came almost every two years. It was on the same kitchen table, off of which we ate together, that she taught me how to bathe, play, talk, and engage my baby brother and sisters. We made them smile and coo with delight and that delighted us. I also learned to soothe them when they were distressed by rocking them in the rocking chair and singing to them the rock and roll songs of the day. I was allowed to go out only after getting them to sleep! All this came back to me as I cared for my own five children and now eleven grandchildren.

Donna (youngest daughter): Yeah, I remember when the kitchen would also be the nursery and I can recall plenty of grandkids as infants taking baths in some of mom's oversized pots! Baby soup! Yummy.

Roasted Red Peppers

Roasted red peppers make a nice appetizer. They are also good to serve with fresh mozzarella. Roast peppers in pan. Put foil on pan. It makes it easier to clean. I would serve these sliced peppers on a pretty dish. Add different olives and some mozzarella cheese slices. Use your imagination.

Yield: a Good Pile, about 10 Servings

4 Red Bell Peppers
1 Teaspoon Oregano
4 Cloves Garlic, minced
Olive Oil
Salt and Pepper To Taste
Dash of Vinegar

Roast peppers under the broil, turning every few minutes till they all scorched, just the skin. After peppers are scorched, carefully put them in a plastic or brown paper bag to cool, about 40 minutes or so. Remove them when cool enough to handle and peel and remove seeds. Now you are ready to slice in strips on platter, add seasoning, oregano, olive oil, salt, pepper, and dash of vinegar.

Spinach Balls

Yield: 12 Servings

2 Packages Chopped Spinach
3/4 Cup Parmesan Cheese
2 Cups Pepperidge Farm Stuffing
1 Teaspoon Salt
1/2 Onion Chopped Fine
1/2 Teaspoon Pepper
2 Eggs, Beaten

Mix all ingredients together and form into balls (your size, you choose). At this point they may be frozen. When ready to serve place in pan. Bake at 350 degrees for 3 to 4 minutes, till heated through. If frozen bake at 300 degrees for 20 minutes. If desired add slice of tomato and cheese for serving.

Cheri (daughter-in-law): I first met the Cusumanos when I was sixteen. Chuck, my then boyfriend, had invited me over to his house for dinner. He told me he was an only child. Imagine my shock when I walked into his house and all ten siblings were home, ages two to twenty! He told me, "I thought you wouldn't want to come over if you knew I had nine brothers and sisters."

Well that day began my love affair with all of the Cusumanos and my great admiration for Carmela. I couldn't believe what command she had over her kitchen, putting out amazing dishes that made my mouth water just walking in the front door. I was amazed how she could cook for such a large family every day and still on occasion make more than 200 homemade cupcakes that Charlie would deliver to the veterans in the hospital. Soon I began taking cake-decorating classes with Carmela. She had such a creative talent and made beautiful wedding cakes for most if not all of her children's weddings.

I will never forget when Chuck joined the Army and Carmela made two large trays of lasagne to take with us to visit him at Fort Dix. Nobody had a picnic feast like us!

Rice Balls *(Arancini)*

This recipe was given to me by a friend, Jean. I was visiting her and she was serving this for an appetizer. As soon as I tasted it, I asked for the recipe. It is different.

Yield: 20 Servings

1 Cup Cooked Rice
1 Large Egg
1/2 Cup Grated Cheese
1 10-Ounce container Ricotta
Some Parsley, Chopped
1/2 Small Mozzarella Cheese, cubed
1 Egg White, Beaten
Bread Crumbs To roll the Rice Balls

Mix rice, egg, grated cheese, ricotta, and parsley. Take some rice mixture the size of a golf ball in the palm of your hand, insert a cube of mozzarella in center and cover with rice, so you will have a ball of rice with a cube of mozzarella in center. Roll in beaten egg white, then in bread crumbs and chill in refrigerator for about an hour. Then fry till lightly brown. Drain on paper towel.

I Remember Mama

Donna (daughter): *You're gonna eat that?* When we were growing up years ago, the American diet was meat and potatoes and most Americans did not venture into ethnic foods beyond cardboard-tasting frozen pizzas or fish sticks, and greasy store-bought egg rolls, let alone know about the bounty of healthy vegetables available. I remember being bashful about having friends over for some dinners. One time, Mom was making Tripe and a friend asked what was cooking. When she was told what it was, a look of horror came over her. "You're gonna eat that?!" Cow's stomach!

Well, actually, I let my friends believe I was. But tripe was the one dish that Mom and Dad never insisted we had to eat.

Another time a friend's face showed a look of pity, that we would actually have to eat the weeds that populated the front yards of our working class neighborhood—dandelion greens sautéed in garlic and olive oil.

Memorial day—ahhh artichokes were our treat then. A friend saw the big green globes by the sink and thought they were some kind of knickknacks ready for cleaning. And, escarole? Forget about eating something you couldn't even pronounce (*scarol'*). These days, people say "you must have good genes" and it's probably why Mom lived to a spry 93 years. Chalk it up to a life-long diet of good food. Granted, Mom never did come up with Kale Chips.

Dad & Mom, circa 1945, just starting out, Elizabeth, New Jersey.

MEATS

Veal Piccata

This is a favorite and simple to make. This can be done with veal or chicken. There are different versions. But this is my version.

Yield: 4 to 6 Servings

1 Pound Veal Cutlets
Flour For Browning
3 Tablespoons Olive Oil
1/4 Cup Butter
1 or 2 Cloves Garlic, Minced, or 1/2 Tsp, Granules
1/2 Pound Mushrooms, Sliced
1/2 Cup White Wine
Few Dashes Worcestershire Sauce
Few Dashes Soy Sauce
Thin Slices Lemon
Chopped Parsley

Dredge veal in flour. Pour oil in pan and brown veal quickly on both sides. Set aside on warm platter. In the same fry pan add butter, garlic and sauté for a few seconds, add mushrooms and stir for a few minutes. Add wine, Worcestershire sauce, and soy sauce. Add some thin slices of lemon, parsley; sprinkle a little flour to thicken if needed. Add veal just to heat and serve.

Veal Parmigiana

Note from us kids: This is another recipe Mom left out because it's deep in our bones (literally and figuratively). She didn't think we needed a recipe and she was right. We worked out a recipe for others' bones and for old times' sake. As kids, we only got to eat this once or twice a year as veal was outside the family budget. Of course, these days, for other reasons, some of us only enjoy veal as a long ago memory.

Yield: 4 to 6 Servings

1 Pound Veal Cutlets
2 eggs Beaten
1 to 1 1/2 Cups Seasoned Bread Crumbs
1/2 Cup Grated Parmesan + Some for Garnish
Olive Oil For Frying
1/2 Pound Mozzarella, Sliced thinly
About 1 Quart of Tomato Sauce (Marinara, See Recipe)
Chopped Parsley for Garnish

Dip each cutlet in the egg, then in the bread crumbs mixed with Parmesan to coat well. Fry in olive oil until browned. When all the cutlets are browned, layer them in a baking dish with alternate layers of mozzarella and tomato sauce, ending with a layer of mozzarella and sauce on top. Bake in a 325 degree oven for about 20 to 30 minutes until cheese is nice and melted. Garnish with grated Parmesan and parsley.

Baked Fried Chicken

This a simple way to make baked chicken and also tasty. This recipe is also good with chicken breast, or other parts of chicken. Terry calls this Italian Southern-Fried Chicken. I make this recipe often, because it is simple and everyone likes them. My grandson Antonio could eat a whole tray by himself.

Yield: 6 Servings

6 Boneless Chicken Thighs
1/2 Cup Olive Oil
1 Cup Flavored Bread Crumbs
1/2 Cup Grated Cheese
1 Tablespoon Parsley

I always soak chicken in some salt water for about 20 minutes. This seems to freshen the chicken and take away the foul taste (no pun intended). Rinse the chicken thighs and dry on paper towel. Put olive oil in a dish. Mix bread crumbs and grated cheese and parsley on foil. Spray pan with olive oil spray. Dip chicken thighs in olive oil then in bread crumb mixture. Place thighs on pan. Bake 375 degrees for about 20 to 30 minutes. If not brown by this time, brown under broiler for a few minutes. Check often so as to prevent burning. This can be multiplied for a large crowd. My mother used to wrap chicken in waxed paper and bake this way. Some of you older children may remember this. The wax paper sometimes would stick to chicken taking some of the crumb mixture, the best part. Chicken legs can also be made this way.

Chuckie (grandson): Grandma made it look easy to make delicious, memorable dishes out of seemingly unremarkable raw materials. Nowhere is this better exemplified than this recipe for chicken thighs (Baked Fried Chicken), a favorite of many of us grandchildren. I would rather have chicken prepared this way than a filet mignon. On the off chance there are any leftovers, they inevitably disappeared from the fridge overnight, but it wasn't me!

Once, when driving cross-country with a friend and my brother Mike, we overnighted at Grandma and Grandpa's in Maryland. We got to their house late, after 1 AM. We found a tray of the chicken thighs waiting for us on the counter, and we ate the whole thing without reheating it, and it was delicious just like that. Grandma always had food waiting for you when you visited.

My cousin Tommy and I have impressed many a dinner guest with this simple recipe over the years. Although not necessary, I like to tenderize the meat first, to make it exaggeratedly delicate. Other modifications that have worked well is adding some minced garlic and/or a dash of cayenne to the breadcrumb mixture for an extra kick.

Chuck (son; Chuckie's Dad): When I was in the army going through basic training at Fort Dix N.J., Mom and Dad came down a couple of times on Sunday and we would picnic some place on base. Baked Chicken worked well on these dates as it did not have to be eaten right out of the oven. So this was a picnic favorite, and as always, Mom cooked more than we all could eat. I always brought the extra back to my barracks. Needless to say I was the most liked and appreciated guy in my platoon but most of all by the Southern guys and African Americans soldiers.

Beef Wellington

This recipe is adapted from Southern Living Cook Book.
Note from Camille: I tried this with a cheaper cut of meat, beef chuck
roast. It did not work well. Do not try it. However, you can probably
cut this recipe in half.

Yield: 12 Servings

7-Pound Beef Tenderloin, Trimmed
8 ounces Liverwurst
1 cup Chopped Mushrooms
2 Tablespoons Bourbon
16 Ounces Frozen Puff Pastry, thawed
1 Egg Yolk
1 Tablespoon Milk
Fresh Parsley Sprigs

Place tenderloin on a rack in a shallow roasting pan, tucking small end
of meat underneath. Bake uncovered at 425 degrees for 25 to 30
minutes. Remove from oven and let stand for 25 to 30 minutes.
Combine liverwurst spread, mushrooms, and bourbon. Set aside. Roll
pastry to 20-x 14-inch rectangle on a lightly floured surface. Spread
one-third of liverwurst mixture over top of tenderloin. Place
tenderloin lengthwise in middle of pastry, topside down. Spread
remaining liverwurst mixture over sides of tenderloin. Bring sides of
pastry up and overlap slightly to form a seam, trimming off excess
pastry. Reserve all pastry trimmings. Trim ends of pastry to make
even; fold over ends of pastry to seal. Invert roast. Combine egg yolk
and milk; brush evenly over pastry. Roll out pastry trimmings cut into
decorative shapes and arrange on top of pastry, as desired. Brush
shapes with remaining yolk mixture. Bake uncovered in a lightly
greased 13-x 9-X 2-inch pan at 425 degrees for 30 minutes.
Let stand 10 minutes before slicing. Garnish with parsley.

Fruited Pork Tenderloins

I made this recipe and found it very tasty and different. I got many compliments.

Yield: 6 Servings

2 2-pound Pork Tenderloins
Salt and Pepper
Stuffing
1/3 Cup Pitted Prunes, Chopped
1 Cup Fresh Bread Crumbs
1 Small Onion, Chopped Fine
1/2 Teaspoon Dried Thyme
Salt and Pepper
1 Egg Yolk
Sauce
2 Tablespoons Vegetable Oil
1 Onion, Chopped Fine
1/2 Cup Beef Stock
1/2 Cup White Wine
2/3 Cup Pitted Prunes, Chopped
Salt and Pepper
2 Tablespoons Brandy, optional

Preheat oven to 350 degrees. Split pork tenderloins in half lengthwise with a sharp knife; flatten slightly. Season tenderloins with salt and pepper.

Make Stuffing: combine 1/3 cup of prunes, bread crumbs, onion and thyme. Season mixture with salt and pepper and stir in egg yolk. Spread stuffing over tenderloin, cover with second tenderloin. Tie closed with kitchen twine. Heat oil in a large skillet over medium fire; sauté the pork until lightly browned on both sides. Add onion, stock, wine and prunes to skillet. Season with salt and pepper, bring mixture to boil. Transfer meat to a roast pan.

If desired in a small saucepan, warm brandy. Pour warmed brandy over roast; ignite brandy carefully. When flames die spoon sauce over and around roast. Cover pan with foil. Roast in preheated oven 45 to 60 minutes or until roast reaches an internal temperature of 170 F. Remove string from roast; cut in slices. Place slices in serving dish. To serve spoon prunes and cooking sauce over slices.

Carmela, middle, bicycling in Elizabeth, NJ, soon to be too busy to ever again hop a bicycle.

Mom with her First Born, James Anthony.
Dad's away at war.

Prune Stuffed Pork Chops

I am always looking for different recipes for making pork chops other than breaded and fried. I found this in a cookbook and we enjoyed it. The prunes and pineapple juice add a nice flavor. This is different from the fruited pork tenderloins.

Yield: 6 Servings

2 Cups Soft Bread Crumbs
1 Cup Chopped Prunes
2 Tablespoons Butter or Margarine
1 Teaspoon Lemon Juice
1/2 Teaspoon Salt
6 1 1/4-Inch Thick Pork Chops, Cut with Pockets
1/2 Cup Seasoned Bread crumbs
1 Cup Pineapple Juice, Divided

Combine first 5 ingredients, stirring well. Stuff into pockets of chops and secure closed with picks. Sprinkle chops with salt, and dredge in seasoned dry bread crumbs. Place chops in lightly greased 13 X 9 X 2-inch baking dish; pour 1/2 cup pineapple juice over chops. Cover and bake 350 degrees for 30 minutes. Add remaining 1/2 cup pineapple juice and bake uncovered an additional 30 minutes.

Grace (daughter): When mom and Dad would come back east while living in New Mexico or Texas, they would stay with me at my Edison, New Jersey, home. Of course, Mom would take over the kitchen. I can't remember what she was cooking this one time but she needed fresh parsley. When I told her that I didn't have any she responded, "How can you run a house without fresh parsley!?"

Then there were two kids, Jimmy & baby Terry, circa 1945

Italian Meatballs

This recipe is for meatballs that you add to Tomato Sauce.
Note from us kids: Mom always loved Colonna or Progresso flavored bread crumbs. If you plan to add the meat balls to cooking sauce, you don't have to cook them all the way through, just brown them on both sides. Feel free to substitute ground veal for all or some of the other two meats. Mom did.

Yield: 16 Servings

1 Pound Beef Ground
1 Pound Pork, Ground
2 Large Eggs
1/2 Cup Flavored Bread Crumbs
1/4 Cup Water To Moisten Meat
3 Tablespoons Parsley
1 Teaspoon Salt and Pepper
1/2 Cup Parmesan Cheese
2 Tablespoons Olive Oil, for frying

Mix all ingredients, except for olive oil. The mixture should be moist, but not so moist that they fall apart. This takes some experience, but no matter they will taste good. This makes about 20 to 26 meat balls. Fry meat balls in pan with olive oil till brown. Add to tomato sauce where they will further cook.

Camille (daughter): I had submitted a chapter from my novel, *The Last Cannoli,* to my reading group to be critiqued. The boy character, Vinnie, incidentally loved food and cooking. My fellow writers thought that this was very confusing, as if it were a red herring, that I was trying to obliquely show he was gay without actually saying so. They wanted me to change that aspect of the character. I was pretty baffled because I was bred in a household where my patriarchal father had very clearly defined roles for men and women (not that I adhered to those later in life). However, love of food and cooking transcended gender roles. Dad had a very sophisticated and adventurous palate and when he had time (when he was not working two and three jobs) helped Mom cook. He expressed his delight and opinions about food all the time. Everyone, boy or girl, developed this reverence for food. I decided that my fellow writers were perhaps a bit too steeped in pure American culture.

Chuck (son): Some of you may remember, when Mom was cooking it was not unusual for Dad to add something to whatever she was cooking. Once when Mom was making red gravy Dad added something to it while her back was turned. Later when we were eating someone noticed that the gravy tasted strange, different. That's when Dad fessed up to adding mustard to the gravy. I still tease my wife, Cheri, that I will add mustard to her gravy.

Camille (daughter): Yes, the mustard! It also went into the meatloaf! Forgot about that. I think I actually liked it. Thank heavens he didn't make us try his ubiquitous Tabasco Sauce. In Dad's later years, it was Cayenne pepper he carried around in his shirt pocket and it went into everything. Then it was ground fennel. You couldn't make one dish without adding fennel.

And then there were three.
Left to right: Chuck, Terry, Jim.

Meatloaf (& Dad's Famous Meatloaf)

Dad liked this recipe and sometimes he liked to make it and add other ingredients. It is good to experiment with this recipe.

Yield: 12 Servings

2 Pounds of Mixed Beef, Veal, Pork
1/4 Cup Parsley
3 Large Eggs
2 Hard Cooked Eggs
1 Cup Seasoned Bread Crumbs
1 Teaspoon Salt
1 Teaspoon Pepper
2 Slices Salami or any other Cold cuts, chopped
3/4 Cup Grating Cheese

Mix all ingredients in bowl except cold cuts and hard cooked eggs. Mix well. If meat seems dry add a little water, Spread meat on piece of foil. On the spread meat, slice cooked eggs and add cold cuts, chopped. Roll meatloaf using foil to help roll the meat, Put in oiled pan and bake 350 degrees for about 35 to 40 minutes.

Dad's Famous Meatloaf: The above recipe is pretty much his, but he would add raisins, a very Mediterranean ingredient. He would look in the refrigerator and see which of our lunch meats and cheeses were getting old. They would get chopped and added inside the meatloaf. So when he made it, the inside was always a new surprise—Swiss cheese, bologna, spiced ham—yes, and sometimes mustard, usually Gulden's. Once he may have put a few strips of bacon on top of the meatloaf as it cooked. Which made it really delicious.

Soon, Mama Mia, there were five kids, circa 1951. (Terry, Camille, Jimmy, Salvatore, Chuck)

Chicken Marabella

We made this recipe the day before Lisa got married. This was supposed to be for guests the day before the wedding. Everyone enjoyed it very much—even the ones that said they didn't eat meat, because this was served on Friday. We also made a large tray of baked ziti. All was devoured.

Yield: 16 Servings

4 Chickens, Quartered
1 Head Garlic, Chopped
1/4 Cup Dried Oregano
Salt and Pepper To Taste
1/2 Cup Red Wine Vinegar
1/2 Cup Olive Oil
1 Cup Pitted Prunes,
1/2 Cup Pitted Green Olives
1/2 Cup Capers With Some Juice
6 Bay Leaves
1 Cup Brown Sugar
1 Cup White Wine

In a large bowl combine chicken quarters, garlic, oregano, pepper and salt, vinegar, olive oil, prunes, olives, capers with some juice, and bay leaves. Cover and let marinate refrigerated, over night.
Preheat oven to 350 degrees. Arrange chicken in a single layer in one or two large shallow baking pans and spoon marinade over it evenly. Sprinkle chicken pieces with brown sugar and pour white wine around them.
Bake for 50 minutes to 1 hour, basting frequently with pan juices. Chicken is done when juices run clear from chicken pieces pricked with a fork at their thickest point. With a slotted spoon transfer chicken, prunes olives and capers to a serving platter. Moisten with a few spoonful of pan juices and sprinkle generously with parsley. Pass remaining pan juices in sauce boat.

Chicken Wings or Drumettes

This is one great appetizer. You need lots of napkins, everyone likes them. Aunt Lily gave me this recipe and many friends have enjoyed them.

Yield: 6 Servings

24 Chicken Wings or Drumettes
1/2 Cup Soy Sauce
1/2 Cup Honey
1 Clove Garlic, Minced
2 Tablespoons Worcestershire
2 Lemons, Juiced

Place wings or drumettes in a shallow baking pan. Mix all the other ingredients and pour over wings or drumettes Bake at 350 degrees for 1 hour. Brown under broiler if you prefer them crisp. If you like them spicy, add some pepper sauce.

Osso Buco

This recipe takes a little time, but worth it, if you want to impress your guests. It is expensive, but worth it.

Yield: 4 Servings

1/3 Cup Flour
1/4 Teaspoon Oregano, Crushed
1/4 Teaspoon Rosemary,
1/4 Teaspoon Salt
1 Teaspoon Pepper
4 2-inch Thick Veal Shanks, About 3 3/4 Pounds
1 Tablespoon Each, Butter and Olive Oil
1 Small Onion, Finely Chopped
1 Stalk Celery, Finely Chopped
1 Large Carrot, Chopped
1 Clove Garlic, Minced
2 Tablespoon Tomato Paste
1 Can Chicken Broth, 13 3/4 ounces
1/2 Cup Dry White Wine
1 Teaspoon Sugar
1 Cup Rice, Raw
1/2 Teaspoon Grated Lemon Peel
1/4 Cup Parsley, Finely Chopped

In a shallow bowl, stir together flour, oregano, rosemary, salt and pepper. Toss veal shanks in flour mixture until completely coated. In large sauce pan, heat butter and oil over medium high heat. Add veal, cook, turning occasionally, until browned on all sides. Using slotted spoon remove veal from pan. Add onion, celery, carrots and garlic to pan. Gradually stir in the chicken broth, white wine, tomato paste and sugar to the pan with the veal shanks. Cover and simmer over low heat turning occasionally for 2 hours or until veal is tender.

Cook the rice in salted water until done. Using a slotted spoon, remove veal shanks from pan and place over the cooked rice. Keep warm. Bring liquid in saucepan to boil and cook, stirring constantly, until reduced and slightly thickened. Simmer for 2 minutes. Pour sauce over veal shanks and garnish with lemon peel and parsley.

Mom and Dad making the best homemade Sicilian sausage, for family and friends, recipe, page 48.

Braciola (Brajole)

*We thought this delicious meat was spelled **brah-jole**. That's how it sounded to our ears in the rich guttural Sicilian dialect. We were treated to brajole only on special holidays. It was always assembled by Mom or Dad, then browned and cooked through in the gravy or sauce, (see page 87). This recipe assumes you are serving the brajole with gravy, in which you finish its cook time. Feel free to get creative with the stuffing the way Dad did in his meatloaf. Anything goes—if you like to eat it.*

Yield: 6 to 8 Servings

1 ½ Pounds Flank Steak
4 Tablespoons Olive Oil
½ Cup Grated Italian Cheese (Parma, Provolone, Asiago, or any mix you like)
4 to 6 Slices Prosciutto or other Ham (cappacola, pastrami)
3 Hard-Cooked Eggs, sliced
½ Cup Chopped Fresh Herbs (mix of parsley, basil, and mint, or just one of those)
1 Tablespoon Minced Garlic
½ Teaspoon each, Salt and Pepper
String for tying the rolled meat
Gravy, page 87

Pound the flank steak until it is about ½-inch thick. Spread 2 tablespoons of the olive oil evenly over the meat. Spread or arrange evenly over the meat the cheese, egg, ham, herbs, garlic, salt, and pepper. Roll the meat with filling up, jelly-roll style, lengthwise—so the roll is longest possible. Secure the roll tightly with string.

Heat remaining olive oil in a skillet and brown the roll on all sides. Cut the brajole to 2 or 3 lengths to fit in the cooking gravy (or sauce). Allow to cook through, leaving the brajole in the gravy a long time—it'll get nice and tender.

Ya don't like my Braciola? Yer under arrest
By Tina, daughter

In the mid 1990s, Jody and I decided to go to an Italian restaurant on Bethlehem's south side with friends of ours. I saw there was Braciola on the menu, something you don't often see, so I decided to order it. Our friends had never heard of this stuffed Italian meat, so without going into too much detail, I told them to order it, and that it's really good as our Mom would make it whenever she made pasta. They both took my advice and ordered the Braciola.

When our food came to the table, everything started to unravel as Jody said it smelled like cut grass and although I thought it was okay, once I had one taste of the supposed Braciola, I thought to myself that this is not at all like our mother's and the the meat might be bad. I did not want to get food poisoning.

I called our waitress over and explained to her that something was clearly wrong with what we had ordered, and that there was no way I was going to eat the dish and neither were my friend. A look of terror came into the waitress' eyes and soon enough I found out why.

She scurried away and we waited and waited for her to come back. Jody finished his food as he noticed that clearly our waitress was avoiding coming back to us. Getting a bit perturbed, I finally insisted she come over to our table again and I explained that we cannot eat the Braciola and would order something else. The waitress, still clearly terrified, cleared her throat and said in a tiny cracking voice, "The owner gets very mad when people complain about her food." I told her, "But I know what Braciola tastes like, and this clearly is not it. You must bring us something else or we will not pay for our meals."

Suddenly, coming from behind me, I hear this rough, raspy voice (think of *The Godfather* with a sore throat) saying: "Where are your people from?" I turn around and there is this haggard-looking old woman with a cigarette hanging out of her mouth, and an inch-long ash on the end of it, just standing there.

Trying not to draw too much attention, I say: "Are you talking to me?" She replies, "Yes, you. I'm talking to you!" Her stare down to me is almost as frightening as her Braciola. Why she cares where *my* people are from—I never find out.

I explain, "I am sorry but there is something wrong with our food and I know exactly how Braciola tastes, as my mother has made it many times. It does not taste anything like this version."

I am pleasant and ask if we could get something else, that would be great. She shoots back with the same intensity and raspy voice she had all along, accusing me of going to restaurants and ordering food and complaining and not paying for it. I say if that were true I would have at least eaten some of the food, and as she could observe, the three of us who originally ordered the food, did not touch it.

I refuse to pay the bill, and after a short time, the Bethlehem Police show up next to our table. By now, Jody is outside and a couple who were sitting next to us in the restaurant tell him, "You might want to go in there to help your wife and friends because the police are there for them." I tell the cops, "I'd rather be arrested than pay for the nasty food." The police officers say they will then have to arrest us because the law states that you are required to pay for the services regardless of what you think of the food. Our friends are getting rather nervous as we file out of the restaurant not quite knowing what is going to happen.

Once outside the police confess that they get a call almost every week from the woman, and that they would never think of eating there or stepping foot in the place just because they would not want to deal with her. In any case, after all of that, the police release us. Phew!

Jody said that he left the restaurant because there would have to be someone available to bail us all out. I guess the moral of this story is to beware of what might happen when you tell an Italian cook that you dislike her food. You never quite know when they will walk up to you and ask, "Where are your people from?"

Homemade Sicilian Sausage (*Salsiccia*)

We are adding this recipe for Mom. She and Dad started making their own sausage after we were grown and out of their hair. They started out with a manual machine, which you can find in many hardware stores. And later they got a major industrial electric machine, which Mom later gave to her brother, Uncle Pat, after Dad died (2004). Dad had a funny saying, "Salsicci' his own," which sounds like "to each his own." OK, you have to know some Sicilian to get it.

These are ingredients per one pound of pork. If you are going to the effort you really should make several pounds and freeze what you don't use immediately.

Yield: Each pound serves 6 to 8

1 Pound Pork Butt
1 Tablespoon Sugar
1 Teaspoon Salt
1 Teaspoon Crushed Fennel (or just fennel seeds)
1/2 Cup White Wine
Sausage casings, available at most Italian butcher shops

Keep the fat in the meat if it is grind-able, said Mom and Dad. Cube the meat and place in a shallow dish. Marinate the meat with all the other ingredients mixed in, overnight in the fridge. Next day, grind the meat and fill the casings, using the manual or electric machine.

Sal's Pollo Convoluto (chicken rolls)

Literally meaning "convoluted chicken," this dish is one that Salvatore likes to cook for his wife or when they have company. He once made it for neighbors in Ohio where he lives and was worried that they might find the stuffing, sauce, and all too rich so he had some unadorned fillets ready to serve also. But they devoured the chicken and left only the cleaned plates—oh, and took the fillets to go in a doggie bag. Sal likes to serve this dish with fresh asparagus roasted with prosciutto and for dessert that famous Italian custard, zabaglione. He couldn't tell us how he makes it but if you are anywhere near Dayton, Ohio, look him up for a live demo.

Yield: 4 to 6 Servings

4 Large Chicken Breasts, skinless, boneless
8 Slices Fontina Cheese
8 Slices Prosciutto
½ Chopped Fresh Basil Leaves
4–6 Tablespoons Butter
String or Toothpicks for the rolls
Extra Butter for browning
¾ Cup Chicken Broth
1 Tablespoon Flour
1 or 2 Slices Prosciutto, chopped
Salt and Pepper, to taste

Preheat oven to 350 degrees.
Cut the chicken breasts in half and pound them until they are flat, about ¼- to ½-inch thick and broad enough to fill and roll. You should have 8 breasts. Place one slice of Fontina, then Prosciutto on each breast. Divide the chopped basil equally over each breast. Carefully roll them up and secure with string or toothpicks. String seems to work better.
Heat the butter for browning in a pan and brown the chicken rolls on all sides. When nicely browned, remove the rolls and put them aside. To the pan add about 2 more tablespoons of butter and start heating it. Stir in the broth and heat. Slowly stir in the flour, avoiding lumps, and

cook until the sauce starts to thicken, about 5 minutes or so. Stir in the chopped prosciutto. Season with salt and pepper to taste—consider the saltiness of the broth you use as well as the prosciutto.

Place the browned chicken rolls in a baking pan and pour the sauce over all. Place in the oven and bake about 5 to 10 minutes, just long enough to cook the chicken through but still be moist.

Rabbit with Wild Mushrooms

Growing up, we didn't have rabbit often but those few times Mom served it to us are memorable because it was truly wild food. Mom's father, Grandpa Catalano, had a friend who hunted in rural south New Jersey. Pheasant, venison, and rabbit were his quarry shared with Gramps. Occasionally, a mouthful of buckshot was an interesting surprise for us kids in this wild fare. Some of us girls thought the lead spheres were jewel beads. The porcini (*Boletus edulis*), known to the French as *cèpes*, are prized by Italians who usually know where to find their own stash of them fresh in the fall. You can find them dried year-round in most food markets these days. Unless you hunt your own, no need to worry about buckshot.

Yield: 4 to 6 Servings

Preheat oven to 350 degrees.

1 4- to 5-Pound Rabbit, cut into serving pieces
4 Tablespoons Olive Oil
4 Tablespoons Butter
8 Ounces Fresh Porcini, or other wild mushrooms, sliced
2 Cloves Garlic, chopped
3 Scallions, sliced
4 to 5 Sprigs Fresh Rosemary or Fresh Thyme, or mix of both
Salt and Pepper
¾ Cup Dry White Wine

In a large skillet that has a lid and is ovenproof,* heat 2 tablespoons each of the olive oil and the butter. Brown the rabbit pieces, turning often to get all sides. Remove the rabbit and put aside. Add the chopped mushrooms and cook until soft, about 5 to 7 minutes. Remove the mushrooms with a slotted spoon and put aside.

Return the browned rabbit to the skillet and dab pieces with remaining butter and olive oil. Sprinkle with the garlic, scallions, and some of the rosemary, thyme, or fresh herb mix. Save some herbs for the garnish. Season with salt and pepper. Pour ½ cup wine over all. Place the lid on the skillet and bake in the oven for about 45 minutes to an hour. Test for Doneness as you would for chicken, adding the remain-

---

ing wine after 45 minutes. Rabbit, being a dryer meat takes longer than chicken to cook. When the rabbit is almost done, remove the lid and sprinkle the cooked mushrooms over all and allow to heat through.

Serving suggestion: This dish goes well with Mom's Polenta recipe, page 148. You should have nice rich gravy to pour over each serving of rabbit and mushroom.

*If you don't have this sort of ovenproof skillet with lid you can brown the rabbit in a pan and transfer it to a baking dish and cover with foil before placing in the oven.

Pasta Dishes

Ziti Baked With Ricotta Cheese
This is another favorite. Instead of using lasagne, sometimes we use ziti.

Yield: 6 Servings

1 Pound Ziti
1 Pound Ricotta
1 Large Egg, Beaten
3/4 Cup Parmesan Cheese
1/2 Teaspoon Salt
Pepper To Taste
2 Tablespoon Fresh Parsley
3 Cups Marinara Sauce, Homemade (see recipe, page 86)
8 Ounces Mozzarella Cheese, Sliced

Preheat oven to 350 degrees. Cook ziti in large pot of boiling salted water until tender, but still firm, 10 to 12 minutes. Drain and rinse under cold running water, drain well. In medium bowl, combine ricotta cheese, egg, 1/2 cup Parmesan cheese salt, pepper, and parsley. Mix to blend well. Put some sauce on the bottom of a 11 X 7- inch pan, then put a layer of ziti over sauce. Top with ricotta mixture and half the mozzarella cheese. Add another layer of ziti, then more sauce over. Finish up with ziti, sauce, then cheese and mozzarella and Parmesan cheese. Cover pan with foil. Make a hole so steam will escape. Bake about 40 minutes or until ziti is bubbly and hot in the center.

Lisa (daughter) I have many memories of Mom and me rolling out thousands of cavatelli with our thumbs. That's how we made them for years—rolling them painstakingly with our thumbs. Mom would meticulously roll out the dough, cut the dough into long lines, and then cut the lines into small pieces. I would then roll each little piece with my thumb onto a small lined board to create just one cavatelli! Truly a labor of love. This was before we found the cavatelli machines at the store called Tuesday Morning. Mom bought all the machines that she could at the store by her home in Maryland and I bought all that I could at the store by my home. We gave one to all the sisters and maybe if you were a lucky brother, you got one. I now use the cavatelli machine. I sometimes also use the slotted board that mom gave me to roll the few pieces of dough that won't go through the machine with my thumb. Homemade cavatelli is something that I share with many of my friends and their children.

Homemade Cavatelli

This is Lisa's recipe. Some cooks call for adding 1 egg per pound of ricotta. It's not necessary but makes the pasta a little richer.

Yields: About 2 pounds of Cavatelli

4 Cups of Flour
1 Pound Fresh Ricotta

Mix the two together in the mixer until a ball of dough forms. Separate the ball into two or three smaller balls. Cover the pieces that are not being used with plastic wrap. Roll out the dough onto a floured board to about 1/4 inch thick. Cut into strips about 12 inches long 1/2 inch wide. If you are fortunate enough to have a cavatelli machine, you can now thread the strip through the machine. If the dough sticks to the machine, add more flour. If you do not have a cavatelli machine, you will need to cut the strip into small pieces about 1/4 inch long. Roll each piece with your thumb on a small lined board (boards that are used for curling butter work great!) or curl each small piece with the prongs of a fork. When done, place all the cavatelli onto a cookie sheet that has been sprinkled with corn meal. Corn meal prevents the cavatelli from sticking to one another. You can either cook the cavatelli immediately or freeze them. If fresh, cook the cavatelli in salted boiling water for 3 to 5 minutes or until they are done to your liking. When they float to top they are usually done. If freezing, put the cookie sheet into the freezer. Allow the cavatelli to freeze and then bag the cavatelli when frozen in freezer bags. Add the frozen cavatelli right to the boiling salted water. They will take a few minutes longer than the fresh. Use any sauce your heart desires.

La Bella Sicilia with Mama & Papa
By Camille, daughter

In 1998, I was lucky to take Dad and Mom back to the old country. I was amazed at how the Sicilian tongue they hadn't used much since their parents had all died, came right back to them. I drove, they translated. Dad, ever garrulous, talked to everyone, introducing himself by his christened name, Calogero (not Charlie), and clarifying that he did not speak Italian, he spoke Sicilian. People laughed at and with him. One evening, the waiters he engaged with stories all but kissed his ring when he told them he had sired ten children. When they asked how was the veal dish, he teased them, saying, *cosi cosi*—so, so. The waiter played along saying, "I kill the chef for you."

One day we toured Dad's cousins' land, part of which was once worked by our father's father. Dad loved seeing the fertile golden field. We stopped in the little farmhouse where the brightly colored ceramic dishes were filled with creamy curds of ricotta cheese just made, still warm. (see recipe, next page) Another day, I was a bit tired of guiding my parents around the ancient Greek ruins and shops in Taormina. As I sat, trying to catch snatches of the conversation, suddenly the shopkeeper and my parents burst out loudly singing an old Italian folk song. It was just the kind of Italian song you would hear as someone played accordion. It raised my flagging energy. I had never heard it before—*Mazzolini dei fiori*—but now I often recall it and that time that I was lucky to take Mom and Dad back to Sicily.

After I left to return home to work, Mom and Dad stayed another week in Sicily. When they returned, they were so excited to tell me about the miracle that they had experienced in Palermo. The cousins took them to the grotto of Santa Rosalia, a 12th-century woman of great devotion to God. To enter the cave where her bones were found years ago, one must go down on bended knee. My parents, although a bit creaky in their seventies, did so and when they exited there was not a speck of dirt on them! How else to explain this but the divine intervention of a true saint.

Fresh Homemade Ricotta

You cannot get this cheese the way it tastes in Sicily, anywhere in the U.S. The cow's milk is just not the same. It holds the blessing of the hay and grass and clouds and the mountain and sea winds that cannot be duplicated anywhere else. All the same, Mom made ricotta often but for some reason she didn't write down her recipe for us. But we figured out one that produces a sweet, creamy, rich cheese. Mom called the resulting curds a "toma." This recipe, provided you use the best dairy products, is as close as you can get to the warm ricotta curds we ate in Sicily and that our taste buds till dream about.

Yield: About 2 ½ to 3 Cups

2 Quarts Whole Milk
2 Cups Heavy Cream
½ Teaspoon Salt
3 Tablespoons Lemon Juice
Cheesecloth

Place the milk and cream in a large pot and slowly bring it to a rolling boil. Stir the mixture to avoid burning. Add the lemon juice and lower the heat a bit. When the curds begin to form don't stir too much or you'll break them up. Allow the curds to form for about 3 to 5 minutes, watching the heat. Let the mixture cool slightly for about 5 minutes. Meanwhile, line a colander with the fine-mesh cheesecloth and place it over a pot or bowl to catch the whey. Pour the cooled mixture into the colander and let it separate for at least an hour or overnight in the refrigerator. Store the ricotta in an airtight container and use it within a week.

BAKED RICOTTA: Oil a glass or metal baking dish and place the cheese in it. Bake for about 3 hours at 275 degrees. Check occasionally to make sure the cheese is browning nicely. The long slow and low heat helps caramelize the cream. When done the ricotta should be firm like a solid block of cheese and it's delicious served as an appetizer with crackers or bread or on a green salad.

—

57

Macaroni with Peas

One day I made macaroni with peas and Daddy liked it very much. So I thought you might like it, too.

Yield: 4 to 6 Servings

Olive Oil
Prosciutto, a Few Slices chopped or Some Pancetta (Italian bacon)
2 or 3 Green Onions, chopped
1 Can Le Sueur Peas, or package of frozen
Chicken Broth, Homemade or Chicken Stock (If using stock, add some carrots chopped finely)
1 Pound pasta, little shells or small pasta

I poured a little oil in a medium pot. I then added chopped Prosciutto, which I bought already chopped. I added the green onions and sautéed a few minutes being careful not to burn. I then added the can of peas and homemade chicken soup which I had on hand. I brought to a boil and turned off the heat. I cooked the pasta (little shells). I drained the pasta and added to the peas and soup.

Pasta with Fennel

This is a dish that was usually made for the Feast of St. Joseph. I decided to make my own version.

Yield: 6 to 8 Servings

1 Cup Bread Crumbs
1 Tablespoon Sugar
1 Large Head Fennel, Fronds Only
1/4 Cup Olive Oil
3 Cloves Garlic, Chopped
3 Cups Chicken Broth
2 Cans Sardines in Olive Oil
1 Pound Spaghetti
Grating Cheese, optional

In a fry pan, put bread crumbs and sugar. Toast mixture, stirring with spoon over moderate heat until nicely browned. Put aside. Cut off the fronds from the fennel bulb. The bulb can be cut up and served as an appetizer or palate cleanser. In small pot pour oil and sauté garlic for a few minutes, being sure not to burn. Add fennel fronds and soup and cook this till fronds are tender, about 10 minutes or so. Add sardines and heat through. Boil spaghetti and cook to desired tenderness. Strain spaghetti reserving a little of the pasta water in case you want to add it to fennel fronds to make it more soupy (a matter of taste). Put spaghetti on a platter, pour fennel soup over it and then top with the toasted bread crumbs. Grating cheese may be added, too.

And then there were nine. (Baby Donna was in the oven.) Oldest to youngest: Jim, Terry, Chuck, Sal, Camille, Grace, Tommy, Lisa, Tina

Lisa (daughter): One afternoon I invited several of my friends over for a pasta-making lesson with Mom and me. We instructed the six or seven friends on how to make the dough, roll the dough out, put it through the pasta machine, and make fettuccine. We hung the fettuccine on a wooden dryer rack that was meant for drying clothes but it worked just as well for drying pasta. We then cooked the pasta with a little butter and garlic, poured some wine, and sat down to an appetizing lunch. My friends who were there still talk about it today. They never got over how awesome Mom was and her love for cooking. That afternoon, my friend, who is *only* half Italian, and I actually got the idea to do pasta-making parties for young kids. We went to birthday parties with prepared pasta dough, had the kids roll out the dough and then put it through the pasta machine. The finished product was served with butter. Kids loved the parties. Parents loved that they didn't have to cook or serve food. We were a big hit.

Homemade Pasta

You can use this pasta dough for any type of pasta, lasagna, ravioli, fettuccine, angel hair, or any smaller shapes. Marcato makes a good affordable hand-cranked pasta machine.

Yield: Enough pasta for about 6 to 8 servings

2 Cups Flour, Unbleached, Semolina, or a Mix of Both. The semolina makes for a firmer pasta.
1 Teaspoon Salt (optional—you can just salt the cooking water)
3 Eggs
Some Olive Oil

If using a food processor place the flour, salt, and eggs in the bowl and process until a ball of dough forms. If it's too sticky add flour. If it's on the dry side sprinkle the dough with a little olive oil and roll it out on a board by hands and knead until it's satiny and not sticky.

If using the manual pasta machine, take a tennis-ball-sized round of dough and roll it through the machine starting at the thicker setting and gradually working the dough through several times with successively thinner settings. This also helps knead and develop the dough. You will know right away if the dough is too sticky, as it will stick to the machine. Simply flour it with your hands.

When ready, choose the shape of pasta you want. We like the fettuccine size for homemade pasta. When you have cut the pasta, let it sit and dry out a bit on a clean cloth or over a clean wooden handle. In the old days, our grandparents laid the pasta on white cloths over their beds until it was ready to cook. You can freeze the pasta once it is dry enough, in freezer bags. When ready to cook, add it to the boiling salted water right from the freezer.

Homemade Lasagne

Yield: About 10 to 12 Servings

2 Pounds Fresh Ricotta
2 Eggs
1/2 Cup Grated Parmesan
1/2 Cup Chopped Parsley
Salt and Pepper To Taste
1 Recipe of Homemade Pasta (page 62)
Tomato Sauce (See recipe, with or without meat, page 86 or 87)
1 Pound Mozzarella, sliced or grated

In a large bowl, mix the Ricotta, eggs, Parmesan, parsley, salt, and pepper. Run the pasta dough through the various settings until you have a nice thin but sturdy sheet of pasta. You will start the assembly in a casserole baking dish or pan about 9 X 12 inches or larger. Ladle some sauce on the bottom, then a layer of pasta sheets—cut them with a knife as needed to line the dish or pan. Next spoon some ricotta mixture on the pasta, layer some mozzarella over this. Ladle a bit of sauce. Repeat the layers in this manner until you have used all the ricotta mixture. Top the casserole with mozzarella and sauce. Bake uncovered in a 325 degree oven for 20 to 25 minutes or a little longer if the pasta seems too al dente. Let the lasagna cool before slicing and serving.

Pasta with Broccoli Rabe and Sicilian Sausage

We have noticed this easy delicious medley on menus in many restaurants these days. We have eaten broccoli rabe since childhood—even in the 1950s when most Americans never heard of the *broccolini de rapa* and when anyone not in the know would take it for a weed. Broccoli rabe, which is a member of the turnip family, believe it or not, made its appearance in America thanks to the nostalgia of Italian-American gardeners, like our grandparents from Sicily.

Yield: 6 to 8 Servings

1 Large Bunch (about 1 Pound) Broccoli Rabe
¼ Cup Olive Oil
4 to 5 Cloves Garlic, minced
½ Teaspoon Salt
½ to 1 Teaspoon Red Pepper Flakes (optional)
½ to ¾ Pound Sicilian Sausage (page 48 or store bought is OK)
1 Pound Pasta (we suggest short ones such as: orecchiette, penne, rigatoni, rotini, farfalle, cavatelli, shells)
Chopped Fresh Herbs (Parsley, Basil, Oregano, or Marjoram)

Wash the broccoli rabe and rinse well. Remove the woody stems—1 to 2 inches from the bottom, depending on how young your vegetable is. Chop the remaining broccoli rabe. Heat the olive oil and sauté the garlic until soft but not browned. Stir in the broccoli rabe. Add salt and pepper flakes if using. Cook until tender, 10 to 15 minutes.

Chop the sausage into 1-inch pieces and cook either on the stove top or in the oven until browned and cooked through. Keep the sausage in its cooked juices. Boil the pasta and in salted water and reserve a little bit of the cooking water. Toss the cooked pasta with the broccoli rabe and sausage. If too dry add back a little bit of cooking water or a bit of olive oil. Serve garnished with chopped herbs.

Homemade Ravioli

Yield: About 8 to 10 Servings (about 60 ravioli)

1 recipe of Homemade Pasta, page 62
1 recipe of Homemade Lasagne filling, page 63

Take a ball of the dough, about the size of a large lemon. Roll it through the pasta machine starting at the thickest setting, number 1, rolling it through each successively thinner setting up to number 6. Any thinner and your dough may fall apart. When you have a sheet of dough that is about 5 inches wide and 2 feet long, slice the sheet in half so that you now have 2 12 X 5-inch sheets. On one sheet of dough, spoon a heaping tablespoon of the filling at each 2-inch interval. Tip: Try using a pastry bag to place the filling on the dough. Gently place the second sheet of dough over the first. Gently but firmly press down the top and bottom dough sheets around each heap of filling to seal, trying not to allow any air inside the ravioli. Using a rolling crimper cut the ravioli out. Place them on a plate or baking sheet sprinkled with coarse cornmeal. When ready to cook, add the ravioli to salted boiling water and cook about 3 minutes. Drain, sauce, and enjoy. If you want to freeze the ravioli, it's best to first freeze them on the plate or sheet and when frozen remove and store them in a freezer bag.

Operation Ravioli

I Remember Mama

Tom (son): I can assure you that Mom taught both me and my wife, Patty, how to make the pasta, especially the ravioli, along with many other dishes. This includes apple/coconut custard pies, etc. For the first few years of our marriage, Mom was our go-to counselor when it came to (Italian) cooking, especially pasta, sauces, dessert pies, pizza, soups, and sausage. Often, some of our longest phone conversations centered around the subtleties of cooking a particular dish. She really is the one that provided the inspiration and my family's passion for cooking. All of my four children have watched over the years as Patty and I worked together to make (in my humble opinion) excellent Italian dishes for our children and visiting family and friends.

Mom & Dad's Ten Adult Kids,
1991, year of their Golden Anniversary
Front: Camille, Grace, Middle: Terry, Tina, Lisa,
Donna, Back: Chuck, Tom, Sal, Jim

Salads

Mediterranean Deli Salad

The classic Italian salad is still served in old-fashioned family-style restaurants. Still good to the last drop even though its center piece, crispy iceberg lettuce, has been upstaged in past decades by many other fancy greens.

Yield: 4 Servings

1 Cucumber, peeled
1 Green Pepper, coarsely chopped
1 Large Tomato, sliced into wedges
½ Red Onion, thinly sliced
1 Heart of Iceberg Lettuce, broken into pieces
¼ Cup Chopped Italian (flatleaf) Parseley
¼ Cup Red Wine Vinegar
1 Teaspoon dried Oregano
½ Teaspoon Salt
½ Teaspoon Black Pepper
1/3 Cup Olive Oil

Quarter the cucumber lengthwise. Slice each quarter into ½-inch pieces. Toss the cucumber, pepper, tomato, onion, lettuce, and parsley together. Combine the vinegar, oregano, salt, pepper, and oil, and mix well. Toss dressing with salad and serve.

Salade Niçoise with Grilled Tuna

This salad originated in Nice, France, the area called Provence, which borders northern Italy, a province that once was part of the Roman Empire. Nowadays, you'll find this salad made with canned tuna. We think using fresh fish is the Sicilian way to go—after all Italians started the Slow Food movement. Note: If you can't grill the tuna, you can broil it instead.

Yield: 4 Servings

1 Pound Fresh Tuna Steak
Juice of 1 Whole Lemon
4 Tablespoons Olive Oil

Salad and Dressing:
2 Tablespoons White Wine Vinegar
1 Teaspoon Dijon Mustard
½ Teaspoon Salt
½ Teaspoon Black Pepper
½ Cup Olive Oil
2 Medium-size Tomatoes, cut into small wedges
2 Cups Cooked Green Beans, cut diagonally into 2-inch pieces
½ Cup Dry-cured Olives (pitted preferably)
3 Scallions, chopped
1 Head Butter Lettuce, washed and torn into bite-size pieces
8 Flat Anchovies, drained
2 Hard-cooked Eggs, quarter
Fresh Sprigs Parsley

Brush the tuna with lemon juice and olive oil, and grill it on an oiled rack set about 4 inches above hot coals for 4 to 5 minutes on each side for medium-rare, or grill to taste. When cool enough to handle, cut into thin strips.

Dressing: In a salad bowl, combine vinegar, mustard, salt, pepper, and olive oil, and mix well. Add tomatoes, beans, olives, scallions, and lettuce, and toss to coat with dressing. Add tuna and toss again. Garnish with anchovies, eggs, and parsley.

Cannelini and Sicilian Sausage

Serve this hearty dish as a warm salad or a hot entrée. Do cook your own beans—just plan this dish a day in advance so you can soak the beans overnight.

Yield: 6 to 8 Servings (as a side dish) or 4 to 6 as a main dish

2 Cups Cannelini (white) Beans
1 Carrot
1 Rib Celery
1 Whole Onion
1 Bay Leaf
3 Sprigs Parsley
1 Teaspoon Salt
1 ¼ Pounds Sicilian Sausage (store bought or see recipe, page 48)
Dressing:
1/3 Cup white Wine Vinegar
Juices of ½ Lemon
1/3 Cup Olive Oil
2 Teaspoons Black Pepper
½ Teaspoon Salt
½ Teaspoon Crushed Fennel Seed
¼ Cup Chopped Italian Parsley

Soak the beans in cold water overnight. In a 4-quart pot, cook beans with carrot, celery, onon, bay leaf, parsley, and salt for about 1 hour, until tender but not mushy. Drain and allow to cool.

Cut sausage into 1-inch pieces and cook. Set aside to cool and drain on paper towel.

Make the dressing: In a large salad bowl, combine all the dressing ingredients and mix well. Stir in the cooled beans and sausage. Serve immediately or chill.

Variations: use 2 to 3 tablespoons fresh thyme instead of fennel in dressing. Add some chopped sun-dried tomatoes for color and zip.

Insalata Siciliana

The fresh garlic in this dish is not available everywhere year-round. So if you don't have access to it use scallions instead—but not regular garlic, which would be too strong. This salad is good warm and if you chill it first, bring to room temperature before serving.

Yield: 6 to 8 Servings

1/3 Cup Red Wine Vinegar
¼ Cup Finely Grated Parmesan
1 Tablespoon Fresh Thyme
2 Tablespoons Chopped Fresh (green) Garlic (or scallions)
½ Teaspoon Salt
¾ Cup Olive Oil
1 Pound Pasta Shells, cooked in salted water and drained
2 Plum Tomatoes, peeled, seeded, and chopped
2/3 Cup Sicilian dry-cured Olives
1 Small Green Pepper, cut into thin 2-inch-long strips
¾ Cup Rehydrated Sun-dried Tomatoes, chopped
6–8 Ounces Dried Ricotta (Ricotta Salata), cut into ½-inch cubes
½ Cup Chopped Parsley

Combine the vinegar, Parmesan, thyme, garlic, and salt, and stir well. Stir in the oil and mix well again. Combine remaining ingredients in a large bowl and toss with the dressing. Serve immediately or chill.

Tortellini with Vegetables and Garlic Vinaigrette

Using a mix of tortellini made from tomato, spinach, and egg makes this even more eye appealing. Use either cheese- or meat-stuffed tortellini.

Yield: 4 Servings

2 Tablespoons White Wine Vinegar
2 Tablespoons Lemon Juice
1 Tablespoon Dijon Mustard
2 Cloves Garlic
½ Teaspoon Salt
½ Teaspoon Black Pepper
½ Cup Olive Oil
½ Pound Tortellini
1 ½ Cups Steamed Broccoli Florets
1 Cup Steamed Snow Peas
1 Sweet Red Pepper, chopped
½ Cup Pine Nuts

Combine the vinegar, lemon juice, mustard, garlic, salt, pepper, and olive oil in a blender and process until smooth. Mix the remaining ingredients in a salad bowl and toss with the dressing to mix well. Serve chilled or at room temperature.

Savory Breads

Dinner Rolls

This recipe was given to me by a very dear friend Ethel Zimberoff. She lives next door to Salvatore and Carolyn. She invited us for lunch and made these rolls in fancy shapes. I couldn't believe that she made them. They are great for any meal.

Yield: 20 Servings

1 Package Dry Yeast
4 Tablespoons Warm Water
1 1/4 Cup Lukewarm Milk or Water
1/2 Cup Margarine or Butter
1/2 Cup Sugar
2 Teaspoons Salt
2 Eggs Well Beaten
5 or 6 Cups All Purpose Flour
1 Egg, Beaten for glaze
1 Cup Poppy Seeds

Dissolve yeast in 4 tablespoons warm water, not hot (about 110 degrees). Add 1 1/4 Cups scalded milk, or hot water, to margarine or butter, cup sugar, and salt. Cool until lukewarm and add to yeast mixture and mix in 2 beaten eggs. Add flour 1 cup at a time until smooth. When dough begins to leave the sides of the bowl, turn out onto a floured board and knead about 5 to 6 minutes, adding only enough flour to keep dough from adhering to hands. KEEP DOUGH AS SOFT AS POSSIBLE. Place dough in large bowl and place in warm place away from drafts. Allow dough to double in size. Then cut roll, shape as desired. Allow rolls to stand in warm place, on pan, until lightly risen. Brush tops with beaten eggs, sprinkle with poppy seeds. Bake at 350 degrees for 20 minutes or until brown.
Variation: Mix chopped onions with small amount of olive oil and sprinkle with poppy seeds. Pat mixture on top of rolls, for a delicious onion roll.

Favorite Pizza Dough
We have used this recipe for many years. It makes 3 large pizzas.

Yield: 3 Pizza Pie Crusts

5 To 8 Cups Flour
4 Teaspoons Salt
2 Tablespoons or Two Packages Dry Yeast
2 Tablespoons Sugar
1/4 Cup Olive Oil
2 2/3 Cups Very Warm Water About 120 F.

Mix about 4 or 5 cups of flour. Keep rest of flour for later. Add all dry ingredients—salt, yeast, sugar—and mix well, then add oil and water. Mix well again and let stand for about 20 minutes. Start mixing again adding a little flour until dough holds together. Knead by hand adding flour as needed so dough is not too sticky. Put in bowl. Sprinkle some olive oil and turn dough over to oil. Place plastic wrap on dough and cover with towel away from drafts. Leave until double in bulk. Then roll out for 3 pizzas and put your favorite sauce on top. Bake for 15 minutes at 400 degrees or till edges are brown.

Terry (daughter): Like all of my siblings, I have a vivid memory of making lots of pizza. While making as many as ten pies Mom would often run out of Mozzarella cheese. She then turned to the fridge and pulled out a block of Velveeta cheese and grated that on the last of the pizzas. Best yet, we all loved it and looked forward to those Velveeta pies, saving what we thought was the best for the last. Talk about American pie!

Chuck (son): Don't forget how Mom would save some pizza dough and on Saturdays fry it up as *zeppoli*, those delicious hot Italian "crullers" sprinkled with sugar and cinnamon, great for dunking in our coffee.

Tina (daughter): I'm not sure what we were more excited about, the Friday night pizza or the next morning's fried dough. I loved to watch her hands drop a golf-ball-sized piece of dough into the hot oil where it instantly exploded. She then put the fried dough into a bowl that had cinnamon and sugar in it. We all gathered around her and asked to be the one to shake the bowl to coat the hot doughnuts. It is such a sweet memory—making them *and* eating them with our coffee!

Like Mother, Like Daughters.
Carmela's six girls. Left to right:
Camille, Donna, Lisa, Tina, Terry, Grace.

Salvatore (son): After a few programmed days of getting uniforms, haircuts, and shots, the real training for the first year at Air Force Academy begins in earnest with standing at attention, classes on the Honor Code, running everywhere, and saluting anything that moves, (the gardener).

But the worst came at meal time. Yes, the dietician recommended 5,000 calories per day for all the calisthenics and long days of training, but the upper class men had their own ideas. I was under the training of a senior that hailed from Brooklyn and seemed to have it in for me, or maybe just people from New Jersey. I still remember his name, but we'll leave that out. Most of my meal time was spent answering his questions on the Air Force, sports, etc. He misinterpreted my New Jersey accent as sarcasm even though I gave him perfectly good answers. He thought he could starve me into politeness.

After two weeks of no communications with the outside world we got phone privileges and I called home to Mom and Dad and asked them to send pizza. In a matter of days, I received about 5 to 6 pounds of homemade pizza. I was lucky that day because no one saw me pick it up at the post office—the upperclassmen were always on watch for 'boodle' packages and would confiscate them for inspection, they claimed. Once back in my room, I hid the hat-box-size package of pizza behind a plumbing access next to the sink. For two nights (maybe three) I shared that pizza with my two roommates and another room of three. It was a feast for all on Mom's pizza. A taste of Friday nights at home, but most all, it helped a lot with that Brooklyn bum on my back.

Pepperoni Loaves

This is a nice appetizer, especially for Christmas holidays. Our friend Margie, Aunt Liz's sister, gave me this recipe. Use your favorite bread dough, or frozen dough may be used.

Yield: 12 Servings

3 Sticks Pepperoni
1 Recipe Favorite Pizza Dough, page 73
1 Egg Beaten with 1 Tablespoon Water, for Wash
1 1/2 Pounds Provolone Cheese, sliced

Slice pepperoni into thin slices. Divide dough into 4 equal parts. Roll each part to a rectangle about 6 X 8 inches. Brush with egg wash. Layer pepperoni slices and provolone on rolled-out dough. Roll up jellyroll-style and tuck ends to seal. Brush with egg wash. Place rolls on greased cookie sheet. Bake at 400 degrees for 30 minutes. These may be frozen when cooked.

Best Pizza Dough By Liz Catalano

Liz [Carmela's sister-in-law] and I would exchange recipes when we found a good one. I like this when you only want to make 1 large pizza.

Yield: 10 Servings

1 Package Active Dry Yeast
1 Cup Warm Water
1 Teaspoon Sugar
2 1/2 Cups Flour
1/2 Teaspoon Salt
2 Tablespoons Olive Oil

In measuring cup sprinkle yeast over warm water. Add sugar, wait till it bubbles. Mix flour and salt in food processor. Add oil to yeast mixture. Add to flour. Mix together to form a ball. Knead 5 minutes. Put dough in a bowl and let rise till double. Punch down and let rise again. Spread on cookie sheet. I like to spread pan with corn meal. Some like to oil pan. Do as you like it. Both ways are okay.

Burnt Spaghetti & Cold Pizza

Friday nights, of course, we never had a meat dish. Sometimes we had sole or flounder breaded and fried in olive oil. Often we had Campbell's tomato soup and grilled cheese (American slices on Wonder Bread). Mom made a simple pasta dish, for which she took some artistic license and called **Pasta Alfredo**: To 1 pound cooked rigatoni, with which she left a little cooking water, she added salt and a pound of ricotta cheese. We grated Parmesan over it and loved it. And other nights, when time permitted, we had homemade pizza the Sicilian thick crust type made in large rectangular pans.

There was always pizza leftover. We ate it cold for breakfast on Saturday morning with our coffee. (We were allowed to drink coffee with lots of milk and sugar from infancy.)

Saturday was usually shopping day. Mom and Dad would take some of us kids to Elizabeth to the outdoor Italian market in Peterstown and all the old Italian shops. If our shoes were wearing thin, we went to Klondike's where the owner (a nice Jewish man named Ray) gave Mom such a deal. Cheaper by the dozen. At Sutera's we got cold cuts, like capacola, mortadella, salami, and provolone. At Saraceno's, we got sesame seeded Italian bread.

Back home we opened white waxy paper and spread the cold cuts and bread on the table and ate, starved after the long hard day of shopping and carting bags into the house.

We often had spaghetti with meatballs leftover from a few nights ago. We heated some olive oil in a dark cast iron pan and fried the spaghetti until it formed into dark brown clumps
that we had to scrape off the pan with a spatula. No doubt the sweet taste came from the caramelization of the tomato sauce. We loved our **Burnt Spaghetti** and were not surprised to meet other Italian Americans when we grew up whose families made the same dish.

Pizza Dough II

I have used this recipe for many years. It makes 3 pizzas, but the children loved it left over the next day and would eat it for breakfast.

Yield: 20 Servings

7-8 cups Flour
2 Packages Dry Yeast
2 Tablespoons Sugar
4 Teaspoons Salt
2 2/3 Cups Water 120 Degrees
1/4 Cup Olive Oil

In mixing bowl put 5 cups flour, yeast, sugar salt. Mix dry ingredients, add water and oil. Mix well, then let rest for 10 minutes. You will notice the dough will start to bubble. At this point, start to add additional flour to make a workable dough. Knead dough for a few minutes till dough is smooth. Put 2 tablespoons oil in bowl, add dough and turn to coat with oil. Cover with plastic wrap and let rise till dough is double in bulk. Divide dough into 3 pieces. Roll dough to about 14 inches for round pizza tin. Add your favorite sauce and cheese. Sprinkle cornmeal on pan to keep it from sticking. Bake for 15 minutes or till crust starts to brown. Do the same with the rest of the dough or make into bread.

Italian Bread

Bread is the staff of life and what is a meal without bread?

Yield: 1 1 ½ -pound loaf

3 Cups All Purpose Flour
1 Teaspoon Salt
1 Tablespoon Sugar
1 Tablespoon Butter
1 Package Yeast
1 Cup Plus 2 Tablespoons Very Warm Water (120 To 130 F)
Cornmeal
Corn Oil
1 Egg White + 1 Tablespoon Cold Water

With metal blade in place, add 2 cups flour, salt, sugar, butter, and yeast to bowl of food processor. Process until butter is thoroughly cut into dry ingredients. Add half the water and turn the processor on and off 4 times. Add remaining flour and water. Repeat on/off turns 4 times, then let processor run until a ball of dough forms. If the dough is too sticky, add more flour a tablespoon at a time. When correct consistency, let processor run 40 to 60 seconds to knead dough to form a smooth ball. Cover with plastic wrap and a towel. Let rest for 20 minutes.

Roll dough into an oblong 15 x 10 inches. Beginning at wide side, roll tightly. Pinch seam to seal and taper ends by rolling gently back and forth. Place on greased baking sheet sprinkled with cornmeal. Brush dough with corn oil. Cover loosely with plastic wrap. Refrigerate 2 to 24 hours. When ready to bake remove from refrigerator. Uncover dough carefully and let stand at room temperature for 10 minutes. Make 3 or 4 cuts on top of each loaf with edge of metal blade or a sharp knife. Bake at 425 degrees for 20 minutes. Remove from oven and brush with egg white beaten with cold water. Return to oven and bake 5 to 10 minutes longer or until golden brown. Remove from oven and cool on wire rack.

I Remember Mama

Lisa (daughter): Every Wednesday before the kids got into school activities, was dinner at Grandma's house. One Wednesday we walked into Mom's home and we could smell something burning. I said, "Mom, what is burning? Mom?" She said, "Oh that new minute rice. I am just going to make rice the way I always make it! The rice caught fire in my microwave. I called the company to tell them that their product is no good. They are going to send me coupons for new packages but I told them to keep their coupons. Ninety minutes is too long to wait for rice." Something was wrong—90 minutes for minute rice? I asked Mom to show me the package? The directions said you cook the rice 90 seconds in a microwave. Mom said, "Oh, I better call them back and apologize." Mom was better at staying with her tried and true ways.

When Mom died, I got a beautiful card from my friend, Elaine Rovazzi. She wrote: "I'll never forget your Mom driving that BIG white Lincoln with your Dad riding shotgun! It was like a floating living room or perhaps more like a "portable kitchen." She would arrive and start cooking with all her kitchen tools! I was in awe watching her commandeer any kitchen! I will always remember her with her warm inviting smile and beautifully styled hair, especially after visiting Tina, her beauty consultant daughter. She was always impeccably dressed, shoes and purse coordinated. She loved shopping, probably as much as she loved cooking.

La Cuccìa (Santa Lucia's Dish)

We added this venerable recipe because our paternal grandfather, Vincenzo (Jimmy) Antonio Cusumano, died at age 51 on December 13, the Feast of St. Lucy. Sicilians love St. Lucy and often pray to her for special intentions. Lucy of Siracusa was a beautiful woman, whose eyes were gouged out as she was being martyred for her faith. Some time later when there was famine in Siracusa, St. Lucy, it is said, miraculously sent ships of wheat into port to feed the starving people. La Cuccìa eaten on her feast day is best made with whole wheatberries. You must soak them and cook a long time until tender. Here is the quick way Mom has used.

Yield: 6 to 8 Servings

2 1/2 cups water
1 1/2 cups bulgur (cracked wheat)
2 Tablespoons butter
2 cups cooked chick-peas
2 1/4 cups milk or cream
Brown sugar or honey and cinnamon, to taste

Bring water to a boil. Slowly add bulgur, stir once, then lower heat and cover pot. Cook 10 to 15 minutes, until water is absorbed. Remove from heat, add butter and allow pot to sit covered for another 10 minutes.

Mix chick-peas with bulgur. Before serving, add milk or cream and heat. Add sugar or honey and cinnamon to taste. Serve hot as a breakfast cereal or an unusual dessert.

Sauces

Pizza Sauce
This is an easy way to make a sauce for pizza.

Yield: 12 Servings

1 Can Crushed Tomatoes
1 Tablespoon Oregano
2 Teaspoons Sugar
1/4 Cup Olive Oil
1 Teaspoon Salt
1 Small Onion, chopped

Put tomatoes, oregano, salt, and sugar in a bowl. In a frying pan heat the oil, then add onions cook till soft. Add to bowl with other ingredients. Stir together and now you are ready to put on pizza with mozzarella or any toppings you like and cook pizza. Easy and good.

Gina (granddaughter): My Grandma made the most fantastic red gravy. My father told me that almost every Sunday they would have a big spaghetti dinner for the afternoon meal. He said the kids would go to an early mass while Grandma and Grandpa prepared the meal. Grandma and Grandpa would go to the 12 o'clock mass leaving instructions for someone to stir the gravy still simmering on the stove but under no circumstances were we to dip bread in the gravy because it was very bad luck. Ah, but who could resist dipping Italian bread into Grandma's red gravy when she had a pot on the stove? I know I couldn't. But she always told us too that it was bad luck to dip bread into the gravy while she was cooking it. Maybe we tempted fate a little. After many years of being afraid to dip (and not necessarily refraining), I finally asked her why it was bad luck. She told me, "It really isn't bad luck, I just wanted to keep you kids away from the gravy!"

Tomato Sauce (With Spare Ribs)

I made this tomato sauce tonight and it was delicious. I will go step by step and hope you have the same results.

Yield: 4 to 6 Servings

2 Tablespoon Olive Oil
1 or More Pounds of Spare Ribs
1 Small Onion, Chopped, Fine
3 Cloves Garlic, Chopped Fine
1 Small Can Tomato Paste
Some Water
1 Large Can Crushed Tomatoes
1 Tablespoon Sugar
1 Tablespoon Ground Fennel
1 Teaspoon Oregano
1/2 Cup of Red Wine
Salt and Pepper to Taste
1 Pound of Pasta of choice

Heat the olive oil in a large sauce pot. Brown meat on all sides. Remove the meat from pot. Add to the pot with drippings the onion and garlic and sauté till soft. Add tomato paste and stir some water into paste, maybe 1/2 cup. Add crushed tomatoes to pot. Add one (tomato) can of water. Put ribs in the sauce. Add all the remaining seasoning except for the wine. Simmer for about 10 minutes stirring once in a while so as not to stick on bottom of pot. Add the red wine. Add salt and pepper to taste now. Simmer till meat is tender. About 1 to 2 hours, depending when meat is tender. Boil Pasta. Drain and pour sauce over pasta and add grated cheese. Serve meat on the side with salad.

Gravy (aka Pasta Sauce, Marinara)

Note from us kids: Mom didn't include this recipe originally because we all know it by heart. It was always gravy to us, until our American friends got so confused we learned to call it pasta sauce. In the old days we drained the seeds from the tomatoes with a cone-shaped colander, ostensibly to remove bitterness. That step doesn't seem to be necessary any more. As for the choice of whole or crushed tomatoes: We find the whole ones are better tasting but you may have to manually chop them if you or your diners don't like chunks of tomato in your sauce.

Yield: Enough for Pasta to feed a Family of 12

2 to 3 Tablespoons Olive Oil
Garlic, a bunch or to taste, chopped or minced
1 Pound Can Tomatoes (whole or crushed)
1 Can Tomato Puree
1 Can Tomato Paste
1 Teaspoon Sugar (optional)
1 Tablespoon Dried Oregano
Salt and Pepper To Taste

Lightly brown the garlic in the heated olive oil. Add the tomatoes, puree, paste, and about a can of water, which will cook down as this gravy requires long slow cooking, say about 2 hours. Add more water if it seems to be getting too thick. You can put a lid on the pot but only loosely, not airtight. Add the sugar, oregano, salt, and pepper any time during the long simmer. This is a marinara sauce, and it is the same sauce you can add meatballs or any meat to.

Toasted Pesto Sauce

The pine nuts or pignoli that characterize genuine pesto were too dear for us to enjoy growing up—except as a treat on Christmas cookies. In later years though, Mom loved this sauce, even though Dad preferred classic southern Italian rich tomato-y pasta sauces. The authentic pesto is made with Genovese basil, but any fresh basil is just as good. You can use pesto on pasta and veggies or as is often done today, on fresh tomatoes and mozzarella appetizer and even on baked potatoes. We varied the classic sauce by toasting the nuts first for a richer pine-nut flavor and aroma.

Yield: Enough for about 2 pounds pasta

1 Large Clove Garlic
2 ½ Cups Packed Basil Leaves
1 Cup Fragrant Extra Virgin Olive Oil
¼ Cup Grated Parmesan or Pecorino-Romano Cheese, or a mix of both

1. By hand: Pound the garlic, basil, and nuts in a mortar and pestle. Stir in the oil and cheese.

2. By food processor: Place garlic, basil, and nuts in work bowl of processor, fitted with metal blade. Pulse until mixture is coarsely chopped. Then, with motor on, pour oil through feed tube. Process until sauce is smooth. Pour into bowl or container and stir in cheese.

Spoon over cooked pasta, pizza, baked potatoes, or tomatoes, or add to salad dressings. Store sauce in the refrigerator.

Seafood

Broiled Salmon in Horseradish Crust

Yield: 2 Servings

2 Tablespoons Olive Oil
2 3/4 Inch Salmon Steaks
Salt and Pepper
1/4 Cup Dry White Wine
1/2 Cup Flavored Bread Crumbs
1/4 Cup Grating Cheese
2 Tablespoons Drained Horseradish
2 Small Scallions Chopped, Fine

With some of the oil, grease a baking pan, which will hold steaks in one layer. Butter may be substituted for oil. Brush a little oil on steaks. Season with salt and pepper. Pour wine around the steaks and broil 4 inches away from source of heat for 4 minutes. While steaks are cooking stir together the remaining oil, bread crumbs, cheese, horseradish, and scallions. Pat the crumbs on steaks and broil steaks for 2 more minutes or till the bread crumbs are nicely brown.

Baccala Insalata (Salted Cod Salad)

You can find dry baccala in most any Italian, Spanish, Greek, or Portuguese grocery store. Sicily is surrounded by the sea, so Sicilians love fish, and especially this one. Dried salted cod dates back to Columbus's time.

Yield: Serves 6 to 8 as a side dish

1 Pound Dry Baccala
1/2 Cup Sicilian Olives, Pitted
3 Stalks Celery, chopped
1 Bulb of Fennel, thinly Sliced
3 Cloves Garlic, Minced
1 Small Red Onion, Thinly Sliced
3 Tablespoons Italian Parsley, Chopped
1/2 Cup Olive Oil
3 Tablespoons Fresh Lemon Juice
Salt and Pepper, To Taste

Soak the baccala in cold water overnight, at least 12 hours, changing the water bath about 3 times, to remove the saltiness.

Boil enough water to cover the baccala and cook for about 7 minutes. Remove the baccala and rinse it under cold water. Cut the baccala into chunks and place them in a bowl. Mix in the olives, celery, fennel, garlic, onion, and parsley. Toss with olive oil and lemon juice. Season with salt and pepper.

Donna (daughter): My interest in cooking began as a very young child and I was always pestering Mom. "Can I help, can I try, can I do it?" One day she was going to let me help make bread. I was ready to dive right in, but Mom said, we had to do things "the right way." She took all the utensils out that she needed first, while I stood nearby, fidgety and impatient. Then she very methodically, measured things. When we proofed the yeast, she told me, "you should test the water temperature on your wrist." When the mixture of yeast and warm water began to bubble up, I was amazed by the magical process. My mother was a magician, I thought. She let me "gently" mix more flour in. Then she showed me how to knead the dough, "until it's soft like a baby's bottom." We left it to rise. I was again impatient and I kept picking up the towel that covered the dough in the large bowl to peek at what was happening. It was a very long process, but finally we punched it down and shaped it into loaves and I was so anxious to bake it, I quickly put the first loaf in the oven. "Wait, a minute," said Mom, "Take it out." What more could we possibly do, I wondered." She took a large knife and made a very faint cross on the loaf. "We always have to bless the bread, " she told me. It was a very early lesson in patience in the kitchen, and, more importantly, gratitude for the food that we were privileged to have.

Scungilli Insalata (Conch Salad)
If you don't find the fresh scungilli, you can substitute the canned.

Yield: Serves 4 to 6

1 Pound Fresh Scungilli
3 Tablespoons Vinegar
3 Cloves Garlic, minced
1/4 Cup Olive Oil
Juice of 1 Whole Lemon
3 Tablespoons Fresh Basil, chopped
1 Tablespoon Fresh Thyme Leaves
1 Teaspoon Salt
Freshly Ground Pepper, To Taste
1/2 Sweet Red or Yellow Pepper Slices
1/4 Cup Red Onion Slivers
1 Stalk Celery, Chopped
Fresh Tomato Slices for Serving

Place scungilli in a pot and cover with water. Add the vinegar and boil for 1 hour until tender. Drain and cool. Slice the scungill into 1/1/4 inch rounds and place it in a bowl.

Add all the remaining ingredients, except for the tomato slices, and toss well. Refrigerate the salad for a couple of hours before serving. When read to serve, pour the scungilli salad over a platter with the tomato slices arrange around the edge. Enjoy.

Variation: Calamari Insalata. Substitute 1 pound fresh calamari or squid for the scungilli. Clean and slice the squid bodies into 3/4-inch-thick rings. Leave the tentacles whole. Sauté the squid in olive oil over moderately high heat, tossing constantly, just until the squid is opaque, about 2 minutes. Remove the squid to a bowl, cool slightly, toss with other ingredients as above. You can chill first or serve immediately.

Insalata di Finocchio e Crostacei (**Fennel & Shellfish Salad**)

As you can see, we Sicilians love fennel and seafood, probably a taste common to all people bred around the Mediterranean Sea.

Yield: Serves 4 to 6

4 Cups Water
1 Stalk Celery, Quartered
1 Carrot, Halved
1 Onion, quartered
8 Peppercorns
1 Teaspoon Salt
1 Medium Fennel Bulb, Thinly Sliced
1/2 Pound Bay Scallops
1/2 Pound Medium Shrimp, Shelled, Deveined
3 Tablespoons Minced Sweet Red Peppers
1 Stalk Celery, Minced
1 Clove Garlic, Crushed
2 Tablespoons Chopped Pimentos
1 Teaspoon Dried Oregano
1/4 Teaspoon Crushed Red Pepper
1/4 Cup White Wine Vinegar
3/4 Olive Oil
1/2 Cup Italian Olives

Combine the water, quartered celery, carrot, onion, peppercorns, and salt in a pot. Bring to a boil and cook for 30 minutes. With a slotted spoon, remove and discard vegetables and peppercorns.

Add the fennel, scallops and shrimp to this stock. Cover and remove from heat. Allow to set for 10 minutes, then drain and set aside.

In a large salad bowl, combine all the remaining ingredients, except the olives. Mix well, then add the shellfish and fennel and toss to coat. Add the olives and toss again. Serve chilled or at room temperature.

Pesce Spada con Salsa di Finocchio **(Swordfish Steaks with Fennel Sauce)**
You can make this dish just as easily with salmon if swordfish needs a break in your area.

Yield: Serves 4 to 6

1 Large Bulb Fennel
4 Tablespoons Butter
4 Tablespoons Olive Oil
3 Cloves Garlic, Minced
2 Tablespoons Chopped Fresh Basil
2 Tablespoons Fresh Lemon Juice
1 Teaspoon Crushed Fennel Seeds
4 to 6 Swordfish Steaks
1/4 Cup Melted Butter
Lemon Juice for Basting

Boil enough water to cover fennel. Add fennel, simmer for 5 minutes, and drain. Purée and set aside.

Heat 4 tablespoons butter and the olive oil. Add the garlic and sauté for 3 minutes. Slowly stir in fennel puree, basil, 2 tablespoons lemon juice and fennel seeds. Cook just until heated through. Keep warm until fish is cooked.

Brush both sides of swordfish with melted butter and lemon juice. Place steaks on broiler pan and cook about 4 to 5 minutes, depending on thickness, basting several times. Cook just until flesh is opaque. Do not over cook. Serve immediately with fennel sauce.

Crab and Shrimp Mousse

This a good appetizer. It's even better made a day in advance.

Yield: 20 Servings

7 Ounces Canned Crab Meat
1 Pound Frozen Shrimp, Boiled and Chopped
1/2 Cup Cream of Mushroom Soup
3 Ounces Cream Cheese
1 Medium Onion, Chopped Fine
1/2 Cup Finely Chopped Celery
1/2 Cup Mayonnaise
1/2 Teaspoon Celery Seeds
Dash of Salt
Dash of Garlic Salt
1 Envelope Package of Gelatin
1/8 Cup Hot Water

Heat crab meat, boiled shrimp, mushroom soup, cream cheese and onions over medium heat. DO NOT BOIL. When heated set aside. Mix chopped celery, mayonnaise, celery seeds, salt and garlic salt altogether in a bowl. Mix package of gelatin with the hot water. Stir then add immediately to celery and mayonnaise mix. Add mix to heated crab and shrimp. Put into gelatin mold and refrigerate.

Soft Shell Crabs

Mom and Dad moved to Annapolis, Maryland, in the late 1990s to be near daughter Lisa and family. Growing up not far from the Jersey Shore, they had always loved the fruits of the sea, but now they had the Chesapeake's highly coveted blue crab in their backyard—or back bay. Mom would prepare the sweet, briny crabs whenever her children visited, when the crabs were in season.

Yield: 4 to 6 Servings

¾ Cups Flour
¼ Cup Coarse Cornmeal
1 Teaspoon Salt
1 Teaspoon Black Pepper
4 to 6 Soft Shell Crabs
Olive Oil
Chopped Fresh Parsley

Combine the flour, cornmeal, salt, and pepper in a shallow bowl or platter. Dredge each crab in the mixture until well coated. Heat a generous amount of olive oil in a sauté pan. Fry each crab over moderate heat until golden brown on both sides. Drain on paper towel. Serve with chopped fresh parsley.

Variation 1: Beat 1 or 2 eggs and dip the crabs in this before dredging and frying. You'll have a thicker, crustier coating for the crabs.

Variation 2: **Soft Shell Crabs** with a tangy easy **Lemon-Caper Sauce**. Make the crabs either way above. Then for the sauce: Heat **4 Tablespoons Butter** with **4 Tablespoons (or ¼ Cup) Olive Oil**. Add **2 to 3 Cloves of Minced Garlic** and heat until soft, but not burned. Stir in **3 to 4 Tablespoons Capers** and **Juice of Half a Lemon**. Stir for a minute. Spoon sauce over each crab.

Easy Shrimp Scampi

Someone asked me for an easy recipe for shrimp scampi and I found this in one of my cookbooks. Simple and easy.

Yield: 4 to 6 Servings

3/4 Cup Butter (1 1/2 Sticks)
1/4 Cup Onion, Finely Chopped
4 Cloves Garlic, Finely Chopped
4 Sprigs Parsley, Chopped
1 Pound Medium Shrimp
1/4 Cup Dry White Wine
2 Tablespoons Fresh Lemon Juice
Salt and Pepper To Taste

Melt butter in medium skillet over low heat. Add onion, garlic, and parsley and sauté until golden, about 10 minutes. Add shrimp and stir just until pink. Remove shrimp and place in ovenproof dish. Cover lightly and keep warm. Add wine and lemon juice to skillet and simmer about 2 to 3 minutes. Season to taste with salt and pepper and pour this over the shrimp.

Even before Mom married Dad she belonged to a club called the Sevenettes. They were seven girls, all Italian, including Dad's sisters, Mary and Agnes. They would meet periodically and pay a nickel in dues, which they saved for taking outings into Manhattan. Sometimes they would eat at Mama Leone's, an old Italian restaurant no longer there. Mom told us how sometimes, using her entrepreneurial skill, they would make little calico "bonnets" for jam and preserves and sell them to make money for their outings. The girls all eventually married but still would meet once a year or so in the evening.

When they met at our home in Rahway, we kids would be dying to know what sort of goodies Mom would make. The "girls" all brought delicious cakes and cookies, too, from the Italian bakery in Peterstown, Bella Palermo, still there. If Mom made her cream puffs, filled with that heavenly egg custard, we would pray that a few were left over for us the next morning. Fat chance.

The Sevenettes also organized summer picnics to parks that seemed so far away to us then, like Roosevelt Park in Edison. Our barbecues included sausage and peppers and hot dogs and hamburgers, some times raw clams and watermelon.

Cousins would run off and play together away from the adults. The men would gather around in a circle and play *Morra*, an Italian hand game that dates back thousands of years to ancient Rome and Greece. The men simultaneously threw out fingers into the circle and yelled a number (in Italian). Any player who successfully guessed the total number of fingers revealed by all the players scored a point. The yelling and laughter always got loud and lively. And the women were satisfied that men could find so much easy entertainment with so little.

Carmela, standing middle, hanging with the girls, two years before she dove head (and heart) first into married life.

The Sevenettes met for many decades. They had Secret Pals and gave little gifts to each other in that anonymous way. The Sevenettes were, in their own fashion, "feminists." They were all traditional homemakers and they kept up a tight-knit friendship among themselves (no husbands allowed at their meetings), which was as vital as any later so-called support or "consciousness-raising" group.

Prosciutto Wrapped Shrimp

I found this in a magazine. Excellent for appetizer. I served this appetizer, then served cavetel', roast pork with string beans and applesauce and salad. Then homemade cannoli and spumoni. That's Sicilian.

Yield: 6 to 8 Servings

1 Pound Large Shrimp
1/2 Cup Dry White Wine
1/3 Cup Olive Oil
2 Cloves Garlic, Minced
1/4 Teaspoon Crushed Red Pepper
3 Thin Prosciutto Slices,
2 Tablespoon Parsley, Minced
Lemon Wedges

Combine shrimp, wine, oil, garlic and crushed pepper in a bowl; toss to coat. Let stand at room temperature 1 hour. Preheat broiler. Drain shrimp, reserving marinade. Cut prosciutto, lengthwise and then crosswise in half to get enough wraps for each shrimp. Wrap a prosciutto strip around each shrimp. Arrange wrapped shrimp in a shallow broil-proof dish or dishes, if you need more than one. Tuck the ends of prosciutto strips under shrimp. Drizzle 1 tablespoon marinade over shrimp

.

Broil shrimp about 6 inches from heat source until prosciutto begins to crisp and shrimp are cooked through, about 5 to 6 minutes; watch closely to avoid burning. Sprinkle with parsley. Serve with lemon wedges.

Shrimp and Pasta Salad

This is a very easy to make and well liked. Lisa found this in one of my magazines and we have enjoyed it with company. Daddy likes the recipe a little soupy, so I add a can of chicken stock at the end.

Yield: 4 Servings

1/2 Pound Corkscrew Pasta
1/2 Cup Thinly Sliced Fresh Basil
1/3 Cup Lemon Juice
1/2 Teaspoon Salt
1/4 Teaspoon Pepper
2 Tablespoons Olive Oil
1 Pound Shrimp, Peeled and De-veined
1/4 Pound Sugar Snap Peas
4 Scallions, Sliced
1/2 Cup Roasted Red Peppers, Sliced
1/4 Pound Brie Cheese, Cubed

Cook pasta according to package direction, drain. Meanwhile, combine basil, lemon juice, salt and pepper. In skillet heat oil over high heat. Add shrimp; cook, stirring, until shrimp are pink and opaque, 4 to 5minutes. Stir in basil-lemon mixture and peas. Cook 2 minutes. In bowl stir scallions, peppers, cheese, pasta and hot shrimp mixture until cheese is melted.

Crab Fondue Dip

This was given to me by a chef who works in a restaurant where Daddy and I sometimes have breakfast. He catered a dinner and served this and I liked it and asked for the recipe.

Yield: Enough for a Party

1/4 Cup Finely Diced Onions
3 Tablespoons Olive Oil
Black Pepper, Salt, Oregano, To Taste
1/2 Cup Sherry Wine
1 Pound Cream Cheese
1/4 Pound Sour Cream
1 Pound Shredded Crab Meat, your favorite type

Fry onions with olive oil and add salt, pepper, and oregano. Add remaining ingredients, mix well and serve with crackers or rounds of French bread.

Clams Casino

This is an excellent appetizer. Aunt Liz and I made this many times and enjoyed them. So did Dad and Uncle Pat.

Yield: 4 to 6 Servings

12 Clams, Shucked, Cleaned and Chopped
3 Tablespoons Butter
1 Large Clove Garlic, Chopped
1 Small Shallot or Green Onion, Chopped
2 Tablespoons Green Pepper, Chopped
3 Tablespoons Parsley, Chopped
2 Tablespoons Pimentos, Chopped
2 Tablespoon Carrot, Chopped
1/2 Cup Dry White Wine
1 Tablespoon Lemon Juice
1/2 Cup Bread Crumbs
1/2 Teaspoon Garlic Powder

Divide chopped clams in cleaned clam shells. In butter sauté garlic, onion or shallot, green pepper, parsley, pimento, and carrot till vegetables are tender, about 5 minutes. Add wine and lemon juice. Mix bread crumbs and garlic powder. Sprinkle over vegetables. Put under broiler till lightly brown. Just for a few minutes.

Marinated Shrimp

Aunt Liz gave me this recipe. Good as an appetizer or with main meal. This is one of Sal's favorites.

Yield: 10 to 12 Servings

2 Pounds Shrimp, Large
1/2 Cup Lemon Juice
1 Clove Garlic, Minced
3 Tablespoons Parsley, Chopped
1 Teaspoon Salt
2 Tablespoons Onion, Chopped Fine
1/2 Cup Olive Oil
1/4 Teaspoon Pepper
1/4 Cup Soy Sauce

Shell and devein shrimp, leave tails on. Mix all the other ingredients for marinade. Put shrimp in bowl and pour marinade over shrimp and marinate for about 2 or 3 hours. Put shrimp on skewers and broil or barbecue. When shrimp are cooked, pour marinade over cooked shrimp and serve immediately.

Grace (daughter): Here's how and what I learned to cook at the age of 12. Mom had gone to work after Terry got married. They told us that they had to re-mortgage the house to help with wedding costs (i.e. buying clothes and shoes for all of us). We had a repertoire of meals that was pretty much repeated on a weekly basis. Mom taught Camille and me how to make the following. (We took turns each day after school, one of us would cook and one of us would iron):

Gravy for macaroni, the recipe (see recipe, page 87) I still use which called for browning 6 cloves of garlic in olive oil, a can paste, a can of puree, a can of plum tomatoes, salt, pepper and sugar. Get that started and then mix the chopped meat for meatballs. Brown the meatballs and add to gravy. That's how it was made back then, usually on Wednesday.

Other standard dishes that fed our family of 12: macaroni with broccoli; chicken soup; salad of iceberg lettuce (the only kind available back then), olive oil, wine vinegar, salt and pepper; stuffed cabbage (see recipe, page 121), and stew made with cheap cuts of beef, potatoes, and carrots; meatloaf (stuffed with hard boiled eggs, any cold cuts, canned peas and carrots topped with onion and bacon if available (see recipe, *Dad's Famous Meatloaf,* page 39).

Mom had a tasty way of making a small amount of meat go farther. Whenever we had chicken soup or beef stew, she would remove the meat from the bones after it was cooked, dice it up, and put the meat in our Italian-dressed salad. Such a simple ploy and it was delicious. Thinking about that salad almost makes me miss iceberg lettuce, drenched in golden olive oil, with bites of meat.

Then there was the time Camille and I forgot to put the carrots in the stew and we were grounded for a week. Our friends were appalled and teased us like crazy for not putting the carrots in the stew! True story, no embellishing here!

I continued to cook these dishes after getting married only I didn't realize that cooking for two did not require the same amount of food! Poor Art would come home from work (wide eyed) and want to know who was coming over for dinner!

Carmela with her six daughters, sometime in the 1980s, left to right, Terry, Grace, Lisa, Camille, Tina, Donna.

Paella Cimino

Our longtime friend and fellow Sicilian, Jeanne Cimino, developed this Paella. A dish of Spanish origin, paella suited Mom's taste for adventurous dishes. Note that Mom's maiden name, Catalano, very likely means somewhere along the blood line our ancestors hailed from Catalan, a region of Spain next to Valencia where it is said paella originated.

Yield: 6 to 8 Servings

6 Tablespoons olive oil
3 Cloves Garlic
1 Large Chicken Breast, skinless, boneless, cut in half
2 Chicken Thighs, skinless, boneless, cut in half
1 Tablespoon Fresh Thyme, minced
1 Pound Fresh Spanish or Italian Sausage, cut into 1-inch pieces
1 Cup Chopped Onions
1 Green Pepper, chopped
2 ¼ Cups uncooked Brown Rice
4 Cups Chicken Stock
2 Teaspoons saffron
½ Teaspoon Ground Coriander
1 Teaspoon Fresh Oregano
1 Teaspoon Paprika
1 Teaspoon Salt
1 Tablespoon Chopped Pimientos
¼ Teaspoon Cayenne Pepper
1 ½ Dozen Clams in shells
1 ½ Pounds Cooked Lobster meat or uncooked Lobster Tails
1 Pound raw medium-size Shrimp, peeled and deveined

In a large skillet on low heat, add 3 tablespoons olive oil. Add 1 clove garlic and stir it around. Rub chicken pieces with thyme. Remove garlic from pan, add chicken, and increase heat to medium. Brown chicken, then remove from skillet and set aside. Brown sausage pieces in skillet, remove, and set aside.

In a wok or large deep pot, add remaining oil and sauté onions until soft. Chop remaining garlic and add to onions. Stir in rice, stock, saffron, coriander, oregano, paprika, salt, pimientos, and cayenne and bring to a boil. Then add chicken, cover, and cook over low heat for 20 minutes.

Wash the clams. Set in water for a few minutes to allow any sand to sink to the bottom of the bowl.

Add sausage to the wok or pot and cook for 15 minutes more. Add lobster meat or tails (t is not necessary to remove the shells) and cook for 10 minutes. If the clams cannot fit in the wok or pot you can steam them separately—for about 10 to 15 minutes. Remove the lobster meat from the tails, cut it into pieces and arrange on top of the paella along with the clams, if steamed separately.

Fresh Tuna with Hot Pepper-Lime Dressing

Surrounded by the Mediterranean Sea, Sicily naturally thrives on seafood. The mattanza, an ancient tuna catch, takes place annually near the Egadi Islands, Sicily's western point. You can read about this brutal yet amazing centuries-old ritual in The Mattanza: Love and Death in the Sea of Sicily by Theresa Maggio. First make this dish.

Yield: 4 to 6 Servings

1 Small Chili, thinly sliced
¼ Cup Olive Oil
2 Tablespoons Peanut Oil
1 Carrot
1 Rib of Celery
3 Sprigs Parsley
1 Teaspoon Anise Seeds
1 ½ Teaspoons Salt
½ Teaspoon Black Peppercorns
1 Cup White Wine
1 ½ Pounds Fresh Tuna Steak
Juice of 2 Whole Limes
½ Teaspoon Black Pepper
3 Thin slices Red Onion, separated into rings
2 Tablespoons Chopped Fresh Cilantro or Italian Parsley

Combine slice chili with olive oil and peanut oil and set aside for an hour or longer to infuse. In a large pot, combine carrot, celery, parsley, anise, 1 teaspoon salt, and peppercorns with 2 quarts water. Bring to a boil and allow to cook for 30 minutes. Add wine and cook another 20 minutes. Turn down to a simmer, add tuna, and cook about 5 minutes, or just until tuna is opaque on the outside, but still pink on the inside when tested with a fork. Remove tuna and set aside to cool slightly. Strain chili from oil, if desired, or leave in for more piquancy. In a shallow bowl, combine oil, lime juice, remaining ½ teaspoon salt, and black pepper. Slice cooled tuna into bite-size pieces and toss with dressing. Distribute onion slices over tuna. Sprinkle cilantro or parsley on top. Allow fish to marinate for about an hour at room temperature, tossing occasionally. If marinating longer, refrigerate.

Soups

Chicken Soup
We like to have chicken broth every day during the winter months.

Yield: 10 Servings

Water To Cover Chicken Parts
6 or 8 Chicken Wings or Thighs
4 Ribs Celery, Chopped
Salt and Pepper To Taste
1 Medium Onion, Chopped Fine
1 Teaspoon Sugar
2 Large or 4 Small Carrots, Chopped
Tablespoon Fennel, Optional

In a large stock pot, bring water to boil. In the mean time soak chicken parts in salt water and remove fat from skin or better still remove skin. When water boils rinse chicken and add to boiling water. Boil for about 30 minutes. Then skim off any scum that comes to the top. Add chopped vegetables and cook on a slow boil for about 1 to 1 1/2 hour. If you like, you can boil some small pasta in another pot. Drain pasta and add to soup, making sure you do not add too much pasta so as to not absorb all the soup.

Broccoli Soup

We made this soup often, but then what is a home without some soup brewing on the stove, especially in the winter days?

Yield: 4 Servings

1 Pound Broccoli
3 Tablespoons Olive Oil
1 Small Onion, Chopped Fine
3 Cloves Garlic, Chopped
2 Stalks Celery, Chopped
2 Carrots, Chopped
4 Cups Chicken Stock
1 Teaspoon Sugar
Salt and Pepper To Taste

Clean broccoli and remove the woody stalks. Cut in 3-inch pieces. Rinse and set aside. In medium pot sauté onion and garlic. Add broccoli, celery, carrots, chicken stock, and sugar. Add salt and pepper to taste and simmer till vegetables are tender. Small pasta may be cooked and added.

If Tables Could Talk

If tables could talk, two of ours would tell tales of crowded suppers as we sat around them and ate many of the recipes in this book. For years, we squeezed around a classic 1950s gray and red Formica table that we opened up every night to extend its length. It was then just barely long enough for all twelve of us to squeeze around it, all of us sitting, by "executive order," in the same assigned seats every night. Every chair in the house, including Mom's sewing chair and a piano bench for two had to be brought to table for supper. Dad sat at one head and the oldest son, Jim, sat at the other. Mom dished out the food and then sat at the right hand of Dad. We said prayers together, then ate in silence until Dad spoke. After supper, we had to close the table and replace the chairs—or there would be no room to walk in the kitchen.

One year, Mom convinced the neighbor across the street, Mr. Nevar, who was an ace carpenter, to bequeath his old table to our family. It was shaped like a pear and had no annoying corners or legs, just a base in the middle with sliding cabinet doors. We could fit more comfortably around it, even when we had company.

That table went to Pennsylvania with Mom and Dad and then traveled back to Grace's home in New Jersey. When she was in college for nursing, some of the students met at her house to study. They wanted to know where did Grace ever get a table shaped like a uterus!

Potato and Leek Soup

I made my own version of this famous French soup.

Yield: 4 Servings

2 Tablespoons Olive Oil
2 Large Leeks Cleaned and Sliced Thin
2 Large Potato, Cubed
1/2 of Small Head Cabbage, Sliced
2 Cans Chicken Broth

Heat olive oil in medium-size pot. Add leeks, and cook for 2 minutes. Add sliced cabbage. Stir for 2 minutes. Add potatoes and soup. Cook on low heat for about 45 minutes till vegetables are soft. Add more soup if necessary. Season To Taste

Bean Soup With Pasta (*Pasta Fazool, or Pasta Fagioli*)

Bean soup is very popular and it is well liked especially on cold days. It warms your heart.

Yield: 8 Servings

8 Ounces Dried Beans
2 Tablespoon Olive Oil
1 Small Onion, Chopped Fine
1 Cup Carrots, Chopped
1 Cup Celery, Chopped
1 Teaspoon Oregano
3 or 4 Cans Chicken Broth
1 Small Can Seasoned Tomatoes, Crushed

Rinse dry beans and cover with cold water and soak for 2 hours (or overnight). In large pot, heat oil on medium heat. Add onion and cook till soft. Add carrots, celery, and oregano. Cook for 2 minutes. Add soup and crushed tomatoes. Bring to boil and add beans, reduce heat to low, and simmer for 1 hour or until beans are soft. Cook 6 ounces of pasta and add to bean soup.
Tip: Canned beans may be used. Add beans after all vegetables are cooked if using canned beans.

Lentil Soup

Soup is the best relaxer, the best medicine, good any time of day. This is one of our favorites.

Yield: 6 Servings

1/2 Pounds Dry Lentils
1/4 Cup Olive Oil
1 Small Onion, Chopped Fine
2 Cloves Garlic, Chopped, Fine
2 Cans Chicken Broth
2 Stalks Celery, Chopped
1 Small Can Seasoned Chopped Tomatoes
1 Teaspoon Ground Fennel
1 Teaspoon Sugar
Salt and Pepper To Taste

Rinse lentils. Heat olive oil in a medium-size pot. Add onion and sauté for 2 minutes. Add garlic and cook till tender. Add soup and lentils. Add celery, and tomatoes and add more soup or water to cover. Add fennel, sugar, salt, and pepper to taste. Bring to boil and lower heat and cook till lentils are tender. I like to cook lentils until very soft, about 1 hour stirring occasional and making sure there is enough liquid. We like to cook small pasta or rice and add to soup.

Lentils, Sausage, and Spinach

This is a souped up version of Mom's Lentil Soup, a bit heartier and full of energy-giving iron. Great for fall and winter meals with some crusty Italian bread.

Yield: 8 Servings

3 Tablespoons Olive Oil
1 Stalk Celery, chopped
2 Large Carrots, sliced
2 Medium-size Onions, chopped
1 ½ Pounds Sicilian Sausage, cut into 3-inch lengths
1 Pound Cooked Lentils (about 2 ¾ cups uncooked)
5 to 6 Cups Beef, Chicken, or Vegetable Stock
1 Pound Fresh Spinach, washed and drained
2 Large Ripe Tomatoes, chopped
1 Cup Dry Red Wine
2 Tablespoons Fresh Thyme (or 2 Teaspoons dried)

Heat oil in a 4- to 6-quart pot. Add celery, carrots and onions. Cover loosely and cook over moderate heat for 15 minutes. Add sausage and cook 7 minutes, stirring occasionally.

Combine cooked lentils and 5 cups stock and add to pot. Cover and cook 25 minutes. Add spinach, tomatoes, wine, thyme and remaining stock in more liquid is needed. Cook 20 to 25 minutes longer, until lentils are tender but not mushy. Turn into a serving platter and serve hot.

Crema di Fagioli con Salsa di Acciughe
(White Bean Purée with Anchovy Sauce)
You can take the shortcut and use canned beans, but cooking your own is always better.

Yield: 4 Servings

3 Cloves Garlic
3 Tablespoons Pignoli (Pine Nuts), toasted
2 Tablespoons Chopped Parsley
1 2-ounce can Anchovy Fillets
¼ Cup Tomato Paste
3 Tablespoons Olive Oil
3 ½ Cups Cooked Navy Beans (1/2 Pound uncooked)
½ Cup reserved cooking liquid (or Stock)
½ Pint Heavy Cream
½ Teaspoon Salt

First make the sauce: Using a mortar and pestle pound garlic, pignoli and parsley to a paste. Blend in the anchovies with their packing oil, keeping a pasty consistency. Stir in tomato paste and olive oil. If you prefer to use the electric blender or food processor, chop the garlic first, then combine all ingredients and purée but try to keep it a bit chunky.

Purée the beans in a food processor or blender, adding the cooking liquid or stock, cream and salt. If you prefer smoother soup force mixture through a sieve. Reheat if necessary but do not boil. Garnish each serving with a tablespoon of anchovy sauce.

Grace (daughter): After Mom published her first cookbook, she and I talked about putting her pastina with butter and egg recipe in the next edition. I'm sure many of us remember this ultimate comfort food!

Camille (daughter): It was baby food! I recall that Tina's husband, Jody, used to be such a picky eater, that when he came to our family gatherings, Mom had to cook pastina special for him. Or he wouldn't eat.

Tina (daughter): Yes, Jody has gotten more adventurous but he still loves pastina with butter and eggs and is still eating it quite frequently. Here is the recipe:

Pastina with Butter and Eggs
Yield: More than enough for Jody or for 6 to 8 Servings
1 Pound of Pastina
1 Stick of Butter
2 to 3 Eggs, beaten
Cook the pastina in salted water, drain, but leave enough water to cover the pastina. Add the butter and let it melt. Slowly drop the beaten eggs into the hot pasta stirring it at the same time. If you like, you can add a little milk to the pasta. Mommy would just add enough to give it "color."

Lisa (daughter): My girls loved this dish. While I was in the hospital delivering Catrina, Vadj was home with our daughter Anna. Anna wanted pastina. Vadj did not know how to make it. He sat Anna on the counter and she directed him on how to make the pastina she loved. She was only three!

Camille (daughter): I told you—it's baby food.

Wedding Soup

I never could figure out why they call this the wedding soup. Maybe they served it at a wedding as a first dish. Anyway it is easy to make and delicious.

Note from us kids: We did a little research and found this plausible explanation at Wikipedia: The term "wedding soup" is a mistranslation of the Italian phrase "minestra maritata" ("married soup")," which is a reference to the fact that green vegetables and meats go well together.

Yield: 8 or so Servings

2 Tablespoons Olive Oil
4 Cloves Garlic, Finely Chopped
1 Head Escarole, Cleaned, Chopped
2 or More Cans Chicken Broth
Meatballs (see recipe, page 36)
1/2 Cup Acini Di Pepe (a pastina pasta)

Pour oil in medium-size pot. Add garlic. Use a low flame so as not to burn garlic. Add chopped escarole and toss it so it gets the taste of the oil and garlic. Just for a minute or two. Add the soup, enough to cover; add more if needed. Cook for 20 minutes. Add meatballs to the soup and simmer for 10 minutes. Note that you don't have to brown the meatballs, just add smaller ones raw to the soup. OK if you brown them first, too. Add pasta, making sure there is enough soup so pasta can cook. When pasta is cooked, everything should be done. Taste and see if it needs any other flavor. Some people also add a can of cannellini beans. Good also.

Vadju (son-in-law): I remember when Lisa and I were dating. There was always good food at the Cusumano's! My first Sunday dinner was a food affair never to forget! The pasta, the meatballs, the bresaola, and then out came a roast! I just knew I had to be part of the Cusumano family! I will also never forget the midnight snacks either! I would bring Lisa home from a date and mom would have a steak in the oven. It was cooking in a marinade of garlic and some other Italian seasonings! The smell permeating outside as I hurriedly parked the car! The steak was for dad but he always shared with me. How lucky could a young teenage guy get? A date with a beautiful girl and a midnight snack of steak! The movie ticket was a small price to pay for one of mom's delicious steaks!

Lisa (daughter): Did everyone know that Mom made stuffed cabbage on the day I was born? Yep, she went into labor and never got to eat it for dinner!

Terry (daughter): I remember, Lisa, when you were born. I was 12 years old. I remember Mom hanging out clothes on the day the stuffed cabbage was cooking for dinner. I can't remember if I helped her in the kitchen but I do remember our clotheslines all over the backyard and hanging clothes outside at times and on lines in the cellar when it was raining or snowing. I remember mom said the doctor discouraged her from nursing because he said it wasn't what the "modern woman" would do in 1956. She had trouble with her milk drying up after your birth and never did that again. Crazy right?

Lisa (eighth child): Yeah, I was the only one that didn't get nursed too! Maybe she was mad at me for making her miss dinner!

Stuffed Cabbage

This recipe takes a little time, but is a great one meal dish.

Yield: 12 Servings

1 Head Cabbage
2 Tablespoons Vinegar
Meat Stuffing:
1 Pound Chopped Pork
1 Pounds Chopped Beef
1/2 Cup Bread Crumbs
1 Large Cup Cooked Rice
2 Large Eggs
1 Teaspoon Salt
Some Water
Sauce:
2 Tablespoon Olive Oil
1 Small Onion
2 Cloves Garlic
1 Large Can Tomato Puree
1 Tablespoon Sugar
Salt and Pepper to taste
4 Small Carrots, Chopped
2 Stalks Celery Chopped
2 Cans Chicken Stock
1/4 Cup Water or Less If Needed

Core the cabbage to remove the tough stem end. In a pot large enough to hold the whole cabbage, put in enough water to cover cabbage. Boil the cabbage with 1/4 cup of white vinegar. Boil till slightly soft but firm about 20 minutes. Cool cabbage, pull leaves apart and trim the heavy rib off the back of each leaf. This makes it easier to roll the cabbage rolls.

Stuffing: In a large bowl mix chopped pork and beef. Add bread crumbs, rice, eggs, salt, and some water. You don't want meat to be too dry, and yet not too soft that it falls apart. This may take a little experience. You will know what to do after a few times. Take a cabbage leaf, put some filling on it and roll it up tucking in the ends into the meat so they stay put and won't open up Repeat with the rest of the leaves.

Sauce: In large pot, heat olive oil. Add onion and garlic. Sauté a few minutes, then add puree, sugar, salt and pepper. Cook for about 10 minutes. Add carrots and celery. Add the rolled up cabbages to the sauce and cook for about 1 hour on low heat, till all is tender. Add chicken stock if desired or if too dry. Keep cabbage rolls covered with sauce. Serve with lots of Italian bread.

The four sons 1991, Chuck, Tom, Sal, Jim.

Catrina (granddaughter): I was lucky enough to grow up with Grandma and Grandpa. I spent many an afternoon with them and I got to help cook and make a mess in the kitchen with Grandma. Grandma and I used to cook everything together. She had a special stool for me so I could reach the counter and help her. Helping Grandma make a creative, delicious mess was my specialty. I also enjoyed cleaning the pots and pans and all of the plates after our weekly Wednesday night dinners. Those nights were some of my favorite times with grandma. I would stand on my stool and be up to my elbows in suds scrubbing away. I even made a mess of trying to help clean. But the following week Grandma would let me start all over again making messes. I was lucky to have that time with Grandma!

Split Pea & Ham Soup

The ground fennel adds a special sweetness that sets this simple dish apart from the usual recipe. This soup freezes well. So, if you don't have a big family as we did, pack the soup into smaller containers and simply reheat as needed.

Yield: 10 to 12 Servings

9 Cups Cold Water
2 ½ Cups Split Peas
1 to 1 ½ Pounds Smoked Ham Shank
4 to 5 Large Carrots, peeled and cut into 1- to 2-inch pieces
4 Stalks Celery, chopped coarsely
1 Large Onion, chopped
1 Teaspoon Salt
1 Teaspoon Ground Fennel Seed
Black Pepper, to taste
Chopped Parsley, for Garnish

In a large stock pot combine the water, peas, and ham shank. Bring to a boil and allow to cook for about 45 minutes. Turn off the heat and let the boiled peas sit and reach a melting texture for about 1 ½ hours. You can also refrigerate the whole pot and complete the soup later or next   day.

Add the carrots, celery, onion, salt, and fennel to the peas and bring back to a boil. Cover the pot and lower the heat and cook the soup for about 1 hour. If the soup seems to be getting too thick, stir in some water to thin it out. Taste and correct for salt and pepper to taste. When slightly cooled, carefully remove the ham from the bone in smaller chunks. (You can leave the bone in the soup and remove it when the soup is sufficiently cooled.) Garnish each serving with chopped fresh parsley.

Vegetable Dishes

Escarole and Beans

This one of our family favorites. Eaten with lots of bread and butter if you like.

Yield: 6 Servings

2 Heads Escarole
1/4 Cup Olive Oil
1 Small Onion, Chopped Fine
3 Cloves Garlic, Chopped
4 Cups Chicken Stock
1 Can Cannelloni or Kidney Beans
Salt and Pepper To Taste

Clean the escarole, taking off some of the outer leaves and any very dry ends. Rinse thoroughly. Bring some water to boil in large pot big enough to boil escarole till softened. Drain escarole. In a pot, heat olive oil and add onion and garlic. Sauté a few minutes and add escarole and chicken stock. Cook till tender then add beans and simmer for about 20 minutes. Serve with lots of Italian bread.

Variation: Meatballs may be added and also small pasta. This is sometimes called Wedding soup.

Short cut: You can skip the boiling of escarole step. Sauté onion and garlic in large pot. Add cleaned, chopped escarole, and stir so that it is covered with olive oil and starts to wilt. Add chicken soup. Cook till greens are done, add beans and heat through. Season to taste.

Escarole, Easy

My daughter, Tina, gave me this recipe. I tried it and I like it for a side dish.

Yield: 4 Servings

1 Large Head of Escarole
1 1/2 Cups Chicken Broth
Garlic To Taste
1/4 Cup Olive Oil
3 Tablespoons Bread Crumbs
3 Tablespoons Asiago Grating Cheese

Clean escarole. Put water in a pot large enough to just cover escarole. Bring water to boil and put escarole in and bring back to a boil and cook for 3 or 4 minutes. Drain and rinse with cold water. Put escarole in an ovenproof pan. Add chicken broth, garlic, oil. Sprinkle bread crumbs and cheese. Put under the broiler for 10 minutes. Be careful that the cheese doesn't burn.

Un-Friendly to Grandpa
By Lisa, daughter

Friendly's is not very friendly. I found this out while taking a visit there with dad, mom, Anna, and Catrina. Anna was about five and Catrina was just about two. Mom and dad loved going to the mall with the kids and me. This particular day, we picked up Anna at school and decided to go to the mall for lunch.

We walked into Friendly's and were promptly seated. Our waiter was a young man, about 16 or 17 years old. He brought us our drinks while we looked over the menu to decide what we wanted to eat for lunch. Catrina wanted the chicken from the kids' menu. The chicken came with either French fries or apple sauce. Not both. Catrina wanted both the fries and the apple sauce. Dad told Catrina she could have whatever she wanted. Anything for his granddaughter!

Our young waiter returned to the table to take our order. We always allowed our kids to speak for themselves so Catrina told the waiter she wanted the chicken. He asked if she wanted french fries or apple sauce. Catrina told him both. He said, "No, I am sorry. You can only have one or the other." Dad intervened and told the waiter to kindly bring his granddaughter both and he would gladly pay the extra. The waiter said, "No, I am sorry. She can only have one or the other!" Well, this did not go well with Dad.

Dad and the waiter started arguing back and forth. Finally, Dad grabbed the young waiter by his "Friendly tie," pulled him into the table, and said, "If my granddaughter wants both she can have both!" The waiter started yelling "Security! Security!" I told the waiter "Are you going to call security on an 80-year-old man who walks with a cane?" Security came and escorted the five of us out of the restaurant without allowing us to eat. The kids were young but they will never forget getting kicked out of Friendly's with their grandfather. It was OK. We ended up at a hotdog stand. And you know how much I love hotdogs.

Eggplant Parmesan

This is a very popular dish, especially now that many people eat less meat. However, if you like it with meat, layer in some chopped beef. Or better yet, layer in the meatball mixture (see recipe, page 36). Cooking time may be a little longer. Just check until the meat is cooked.

Yield: 6 to 8 servings

1 Large Eggplant
1 Small Mozzarella
3 to 4 Cups Tomato Sauce (See recipe, page 86)
Parmesan Cheese
Salt
Oil For Frying or Baking

Peel eggplant, slice about 1/4-inch thick. Layer slices in colander as you salt them lightly. This enables the bitter juices to extract. Cover with a dish and let stand for about 30 minutes or so. Rinse and squeeze eggplant and dry on paper towel. At this point you can fry in oil till lightly brown or you can brush slices with oil and bake on baking sheet. This is a matter of taste. Frying takes a lot of oil. They should be drained on paper towel. In casserole put some sauce on the bottom, then layer eggplant, put some sauce on eggplant, then some sliced mozzarella and grated Parmesan cheese. Do the same with the rest of eggplant until finished. Cover casserole and bake till cheese melts and all is hot about 20 to 30 minutes.

Variation: This will be much richer but you can dip the eggplant slices first in egg then in seasoned bread crumbs, fry in olive oil, then proceed with the layering in a casserole as above. Delicious but more calories.

Green Fried Peppers

Everyone likes fried peppers with onions. Sometimes Italian sausage may be added and also potatoes. Chuck's wife, Cheri, likes to mix in red and yellow peppers. The sharper-tasting green peppers are not yet ripe and yellow and red are sweeter with degrees of ripeness. Chuck likes to make a dish called Chicken Murphy that calls for peppers and onions, which he will share only with anyone who dares to go camping with him.

Yield: 4 Servings

1/4 Cup Olive Oil, or More If Needed
4 Large Green Peppers, Sliced
1 Large Onion, Sliced
1 Teaspoon Salt or More
1 Teaspoon Black Pepper
1/2 Teaspoon Ground Fennel (optional)
1/4 Cup Wine Vinegar
1 Tablespoon Ground Fennel, optional

Heat the oil in a fry pan and add peppers and onions. Season with salt, pepper and fennel if using it. Cook, stirring and watching they don't burn. Cook till peppers are soft. Turn off the heat and add the vinegar.

Variations:

Sausage, Peppers, and Potatoes: As Mom notes above you place sliced green peppers, onions, sliced potatoes, sausage and the seasonings—maybe add some oregano too—in a big pan or baking dish and cook all in an oven, about 350 degrees until the sausage is cooked, 45 minutes to an hour. Then add the vinegar; the tart acid is a really nice touch to what may seem pedestrian fare.

Peppers and Eggs: To the above Green Fried Peppers, when fully cooked, reheat in a pan with however many beaten eggs you want. This is not an omelet so don't worry about the eggs looking pretty. Make sandwiches, hot or cold. Use Italianbread and let it soak up the olive oil juices. Carmela'sgranddaughters love the sandwiches either way.

String Bean Salad, Old-Style

In her first version of this book, Mom left out these two basic vegetable dishes that we ate frequently when growing up in New Jersey. For old time's sake, we are including them. This dressing is exactly the same as what we tossed our frequent salad served with our macaroni dishes—crisp iceberg lettuce, tomatoes, onions, canned olives dressed like the string beans below. It's the salad you get in mid-range Italian restaurants, although they may serve a bottled dressing with cornstarch. It's so easy to make your own fresh.

Yields: 4 to 6 Servings

1 Can of French-cut Green String Beans, drained, Or, if you prefer, 2 Cups Cooked Fresh String Beans, cut French style.
2 Tablespoons Wine Vinegar
1/4 Cup Olive Oil
1/2 Teaspoon Minced Garlic (or less)
1 Teaspoon Dried Oregano
Salt and Pepper To Taste

Toss all together and let it marinate about 30 minutes. Serve chilled or at room temperature.

Peas With Bacon & Onions

We still love this side dish with the American part of our Thanksgving feast (which always comes after the ravioli). You can use Pancetta in place of bacon.

2 to 3 Strips of Bacon, sliced into small pieces
Olive oil if necessary
1 Small Onion, diced
1 Package Frozen Peas

Brown the bacon for about 5 to 7 minutes, then stir in the onion, adding a little olive oil if too dry. Cook enough so that onion is soft and bacon is crispy but don't burn the onions. Stir in the peas, cover the pot and let them heat through.

Mushrooms, Stuffed

Our holiday wasn't complete without our stuffed mushrooms.

Yield: 8 to 10 Servings as sided dish

1 Pound Large Mushroom Caps, stems removed
1/2 Cup Flavored Bread Crumbs
1/2 Cup Parmesan Cheese
1 Clove Minced Garlic, or 1/2 Teaspoon Granulated
1/4 Cup, or More Olive Oil

Wipe mushrooms of any grit and remove caps and discard or add to soups or stews. Combine bread crumbs, cheese, and garlic. Fill mushroom caps with bread crumbs mixture. Drizzle some olive oil on each cap. Bake at 375 degrees for 15-20 minutes. Serve as side vegetable dish.

Variation: Take 2 strips bacon, finely chopped and fry till crisp. Add to bread crumbs and stuff mushrooms.

Lisa (daughter): Mom lived near us in Maryland for 14 years. There were many times when we would travel to New Jersey or other places for a celebration. My girls, Anna and Catrina, would ask as we traveled over the Chesapeake Bay Bridge to Grandma's house, "Do you think Grandma will bring the pepper-and-egg sandwiches?" Mom always got in the car with her small suitcase and a huge bag of food. The bag always had the pepper-and-egg sandwiches made on delicious Italian bread, some fruit (usually a banana), and some kind of sweet that she made! The kids loved the sandwiches and Mom said they were good for traveling because they didn't need to be kept cold.

MAM + AUNT RITA

Vintage Carmela, 1930s

Zucchini

Yield: 6 Servings

2 Tablespoons Olive Oil
1 Medium Onion, Chopped Fine
4 Medium Zucchini
4 Small Carrots, Peeled and Cut into Coins
1/4 Piece Red Pepper, Optional
1 Small Can Seasoned Tomatoes, Crushed
Chopped Basil, Ground Fennel, optional
1 Teaspoon sugar
Salt and Pepper

In medium-size pan pour olive oil, sauté onion. Peel zucchini and quarter and cut into 1-inch pieces. Add zucchini to onions. Add carrots and red pepper and crushed tomatoes. Add some chopped basil, ground fennel, if desired. Add sugar and salt and pepper to taste. Cover and cook on medium heat until tender, about 7 to 10 minutes.
Serving suggestion: You can cook some small pasta and add to zucchini or you can add some eggs. Break eggs over zucchini and poach. Serve with bread.

Cucuzza
Note from us: We never ate zucchini as kids. We ate cucuz', (sounds like goo-gootz) that bright green, crooked-neck squash that you could only grow in your grandma's garden—well, back then—or was available at the only Italian market for miles around.

To make Cucuz': Sauté a chopped onion in olive oil, add chopped cucuzza, a large can of good tomatoes, or a bunch of chopped fresh ones, season with salt, pepper, oregano, or fresh basil. Simmer till all is tender. You can add bell pepper to the onion, if you like. The French based their ratatouille on this dish. Ratatouille is Provençale, Provence being an area of France that was once Italian and still maintains a large Italian influence in its cooking and warm hospitality—and its musical dialect.

We Remember the Italian Market, Peterstown, Elizabeth, NJ

Chuck (son): You could buy a live chicken at Sutera's in the Peterstown Italian market. While you went to finish your shopping, they would kill and clean the chicken for you. Jim did work there selling eggs on Saturday.

Jim (son): Yes, I worked every Saturday there for Charlie the Egg Man, whose stand was located just outside of that chicken store. That was a great Italian grocery store, Sutera's, right across the street. I went there every Saturday with Grandma Cusumano or Mom and Dad. Sutera's had all of the best imports from Sicily. You could smell the ripe cheeses, cured meats, the *bacala* (dried salted cod) and everything good.

I also used to invite my friends to join me on my breaks from Charlie's stand and we would go into the chicken store, watch them decapitate the poor poultry, stick their torsos in boiling hot water and then hold them to a rapidly spinning large wire brush that removed all of their feathers. I always thought it would make a great documentary movie! *Yuk!*

As for Charlie the Egg Man, he was a nice guy though not Italian. He had a chicken farm in Lakewood, but the most significant thing I recall was that every Saturday at 3 PM, shortly before the market closed, a big Italian guy came by and Charlie and he went into the cab of the egg truck. Charlie told me to take over. The two men seemed to be up to something very secret. Every Saturday, it was the same routine. Curiosity got the best of me. One Saturday, I decided to sneak on them to see what they were doing. Early in the morning, I positioned the truck's side mirrors so that I could see what they were up to. I thought it was gambling or a numbers racket. Nothing that exciting. Charlie, being a relatively introverted guy and afraid to go face–to–face with a druggist, was buying a dozen Trojan prophylactics from the guy. I don't know if he used them all every week, but he sure kept buying them—every Saturday! Wow, the things introverts do—or rather, can do!

Tom (son): I am old enough to remember the chicken store. The one thing that stands out in my memory is all the noise the chickens would make while in the cages. But, when a chicken was taken out of a cage ready to be beheaded, it went silent, as if it knew what was going on or wondering who was next.

How many Sicilians does it take to have a party? If you look closely you can count 17 bodies (or body parts) in this early 1960s photo. And, they are gathered in our cellar in Rahway, in an area about 8 X 9 feet. The odd part is that it appears that all are actually listening to one person (that hand) tell a story. A rare moment of calm.

Cauliflower, Baked

My daughter, Tina, gave me this recipe and I added some garlic to it. It is very simple and nice.

Yield: 6 Servings

1 Head Cauliflower
1/4 Cup Olive Oil
2 Cloves Garlic, Chopped
Salt and Pepper To Taste

Clean cauliflower and break into florets and wash. Put cauliflower in casserole, sprinkle olive oil over cauliflower and chopped garlic. Set oven at 400 degrees, and cook for 20 minutes or until cauliflower is tender. Season to taste. *Serving suggestion:* You may boil some pasta and pour cauliflower over pasta with grated cheese. Very good and easy.

Eggplant Sandwiches

I adapted this from Recipes by Carlo Middione. His recipes are simple and easy to follow and taste good.

Yield: About 8 to 12 Servings, depending on eggplant

1 Eggplant
8 to 12 Thin Slices of Mortadella or Capacola
8 to 12 Thin Slices of Provolone Cheese
2 Large Eggs
1/2 Cup Seasoned Bread Crumbs
1/4 Cup Grated Parmesan
3 Tablespoons Parsley
Olive Oil For Drizzling On Sandwiches

Slice the eggplant crosswise about ¼-inch thick. Lightly salt the slices, let them drain in a colander under a 2-pound weight for an hour, then pat them dry with paper towels. Place a slice of Mortadella in a single layer between each 2 slices of eggplant. Do the same with the Provolone, placing it over the Mortadella in each of the sandwiches. Put the other slice of eggplant on top. Beat the eggs in a shallow dish. Mix together the bread crumbs, grated cheese, and parsley in a shallow dish. Dip the sandwiches first into the beaten egg, coating them evenly and well, then into the plate of mixed crumbs, cheese and parsley, being sure to blanket the edges of the sandwiches as well as the tops and bottom with the crumb mixture. Drizzle on about 1 teaspoon of extra virgin olive oil over the top and bottom of each sandwich. Arrange them on a greased baking sheet and place in a preheated 375 degree oven for 35 minutes or until they are golden brown and crispy. Turn them once during the cooking cycle. The eggplant sandwiches are delicious cut into wedges and served with drinks at cocktail time. They are good at room temperature.

We invented Garlicky Greens

This image is a venerable sensory awakening: We see Mom quietly stirring around the kitchen, very focused, almost as if praying as she works. She uses a can opener to poke holes in a gallon can of Gemma olive oil. She pours a generous stream of the golden liquid into a dented pot on the stove, then adds the minced garlic. The smell tickles our noses as we await Dad's return from work so we can eat supper, almost never before 6 PM. All of our friends eat at 5 PM. The aroma is a commonplace for us but unique to our home in the waspish neighborhood. Now we hear a loud sizzle as Mom drops boiled dark greens into the hot oil.

Today we know that dark greens have lots of vitamins and minerals. They are good for the liver, a cleanser for that vital organ, at least that's what the old Sicilians told us. (Anisette, Fernet Branca, Cynar—these too were good for digestion and the liver, we never asked why.)

Today, garlicky greens are common on restaurant menus. And you find all the greens that our grandparents grew in their gardens. **Spinach** and **Swiss chard** are common. But also try **dandelion** greens. Mom has included her recipes for **escarole**, also known as *cicoria* or **chicory**. And of course, today you can infuse **kale, collards, turnip** and **beet greens** with garlic and olive oil. You can make garlicky greens either of two ways. You can boil the greens in water, drain, and then add to sautéed garlic and olive oil. Or you can rinse the greens well and allow the water that still clings to them to help them cook in the garlicky olive oil. A third option is to cook the green, however you like and simply pour sautéed garlic and olive oil over the greens in a serving dish. Try mixing different greens, allowing that some, like kale, take a little longer to cook.

Broccoli and **broccoli rabe** (not related to each other, the latter is *rapini)*, are also delicious with this garlic-olive oil treatment. We don't recommend mixing broccoli rabe with other greens. It has a strong, pungent flavor and is best enjoyed alone. Be sure to cut away the woody stems. Boil this vegetable first, then sauté with garlic and olive oil. It's great with pasta or pasta and sausage.

Another day, another feast in la Cucina di Carmela.

Asparagus and Mushrooms

Yield: 4 to 6 Servings

1 Pound Asparagus
1/2 Pound Mushrooms
3 Green Onions
1/4 Cup Olive Oil
Salt and Pepper, To Taste

Clean asparagus by snapping off the ends that are tough. Rinse off and put in boiling water for about 3 minutes. Drain and put aside. Slice onions and sauté in olive oil for a minute. Add cleaned mushrooms and cook for 2 minutes on medium heat. Add asparagus stirring till everything is heated through. Season to taste.

Lisa (daughter): We were traveling from LAX Airport to Ojai, for the millennium celebration and Dad's 80th at our brother Jim's. We stopped somewhere along the Pacific Ocean for lunch. I was reading the menu to my daughter Catrina, who at the time was only two. I will never forget the look on the waitress's face when Catrina told the waitress that she wanted the broccoli rabe (or *rapini*). When the waitress asked Catrina how she knew about the broccoli rabe, Catrina said, "My grandma makes it all the time and I love the way she makes it!"

Carmela, right, in her Easter bonnet with some frills upon it, 1940s.

Stuffed Eggplant with Tomato Sauce

Yield: 6 to 8 Servings

1 Large Eggplant
Sauce:
Olive Oil
1 Small Onion
1 or 2 Cloves Garlic
1 Can Crushed Tomatoes
1 Tablespoon Sugar
1 Tablespoon Fennel, ground (optional)
Salt and Pepper, To Taste
Stuffing:
1 Pound Ricotta Cheese
1/3 Cup Grated Parmesan
1 Egg
1 Teaspoon Parsley
1 Teaspoon Salt
1/2 Teaspoon Black Pepper

Peel eggplant, slice and salt lightly and layer in colander for about 30 minutes. Rinse and pat dry on paper toweling. Fry, broil, or grill the eggplant. Whichever way you choose, first brush the eggplant slices on both sides with some olive oil, using a pastry brush. When brown or soft, remove eggplant and put aside. Eggplant does not have to be thoroughly cooked, as it will cook more when you assemble it with the stuffing and sauce.

Make the Sauce: Pour a little olive oil in a sauce pot. Sauté onion and garlic, be sure not to let burn. Add tomatoes and seasoning and cook slowly for about 30 to 40 minutes.

Stuffing: Mix the ricotta, grated cheese, egg, parsley, and salt and pepper.

Assemble: In a baking pan layer sauce, then eggplant ricotta mixture, and more eggplant, then sauce. Continue on till all ingredients are used. Cover and bake 40 minutes at 350 degrees. This is almost like making lasagna, except that you use the eggplant instead of pasta! Serve with crusty Italian bread.

I Remember Papa

Tina (daughter): When we were living in Ringtown, PA, and Dad was retired, he made my school lunch for me. Obviously, plying his creative approach to food, he made some of the best sandwiches, including lots of my favorites. One of Dad's best sandwiches was tuna dressed with olive oil and roasted peppers. He would add a little lemon juice and black pepper, and put it on some good Italian bread. It was delicious. Dad always put our nicknames (mine was Pinky, Donna was Wimpy or Whimpus) in black magic marker on the front of the bag with an affectionate message like "You know I love ya!" I was never embarrassed to let anyone see my lunch bag, though Donna was and hid hers.

One afternoon when I came home from school, Dad was sitting at the kitchen table reading the newspaper. He asked me how I enjoyed my lunch that that day. I hesitated but then told him, "My lunch was stolen out of my locker!"

Well he got the look on his face that I knew well. It meant he was really mad (who has not experienced that *look*?). Then he got calm and told me he was going to make me a lunch for the next day but not to eat it. I was dying to ask him why, but if you knew our father you knew to never question him. You just did as told. So I went to school the next day like usual, put my lunch in my locker, and went about my day. When I went to check my locker, and just like the day before, it was gone.

When I came home from school and told Dad that it was stolen again, he told me I wouldn't have to worry about my lunch being stolen again. So at this point, I had to ask, "How are you so sure?" He didn't say a word. He just showed me his homemade hot pepper flakes. He made my sandwich as usual, and this time he put his hot pepper flakes inconspicuously into the sandwich. Now those red hot peppers flakes were extremely *hot,* so all I can say is to this day that I feel sorry for the person who stole my lunches! And as usual, Dad was right. My lunch was never again stolen.

Braised Fennel

We always had fresh slices of fennel at Thanksgiving when we were apt to eat too much. We seldom cooked it, as it is a great appetizer raw. But here is a delicious way to cook the fennel bulb. Slice the bulb and in a baking dish cover the slices with half beef or chicken broth and half Marsala. Braise in a 350-degree oven for about 30 minutes or until the fennel is tender. Serve it on an appetizer tray with olives and roasted peppers.

I Remember Grandma

Camille (daughter): Years ago, Grandma Cusumano, Dad's Mom, visited me in San Francisco with her daughter, our Aunt Jenny. On our way to Napa and Sonoma wine country, we stopped for a rest. Suddenly Grandma was waddling off into a field, turning her cotton checkered dress into an apron that she began to fill with weeds. Grandma, who lived in New Jersey, hadn't seen a field of wild fennel (different from bulb fennel) since her girlhood in Sicily. That evening Grandma soaked the tender fennel fronds, which she called *finocch'*, in salted water to remove bitterness. The next day she made a classic tomato sauce, mashing in a can of crushed anchovies. She pan toasted a mix of bread crumbs and grated Parmesan until brown. She sautéed the drained fennel in garlic and olive oil, cooked spaghetti, tossed it with sauce and the fennel and topped each serving with the toasted crumb-cheese mixture. She regaled a half-dozen of my friends that evening. I never told my one vegetarian friend about the anchovies. For years Mom and Dad had a snapshot of smiling Grandma proffering her bunch of wild fennel to Aunt Jenny. Both are deceased but I'll never forget the recipe for **Grandma Cusumano's Spaghet' con Finocch'.** Try it—especially if you live in Northern California where the fennel grows like a weed and its delicate licorice scent fills the air.

Stuffed Artichokes

Yield: 2 to 4 Servings as an appetizer

2 Large Artichokes
1/2 Cup Flavored Bread Crumbs
1/2 Cup Parmesan Cheese
1 Tablespoon Parsley
1 Clove Garlic, chopped
1/2 Teaspoon Salt
1/4 Teaspoon Black Pepper
Olive Oil

Clean artichokes. Cut off stems, remove any brown outer leaves, trim about an inch off the top. Careful not to stick yourself. Spread the leaves open gently and put in some acidulated water (water with some lemon juice in it) to keep them from getting dark. In a small dish mix the bread crumbs, cheese, parsley, garlic, salt, and pepper. I also add another clove of garlic or two to the cooking water for more flavor. Cook till the leaves are tender, that is, they come off easily when you pull one, about 30 to 40 minutes depending on how tender the chokes are to begin with, and their size.

Grandma Cusumano's Cardoon Cutlets

Cardoons (*god-dunes*) *make you think of a sweater—cardigan, but the way our parents and grandparents pronounced the Sicilian, cardun', it sounded like god-dunes to our ears. Cardoons are a thistle, a wild artichoke actually. Where Mom and Dad grew up, Peterstown in Elizabeth, New Jersey, the old-timers all had their secret patch of weeds where they harvested cardoons. You could also buy them in the Italian market. Dad's Mom, Grandma Cusumano, made them the best. We give you her recipe here.*

Yield: 8 to 10 Servings

1 1/2 to 2 pounds cardoons
1 Teaspoon Salt
3 to 4 Large Eggs
1 to 1 1/2 Cups Seasoned Bread Crumbs
Olive Oil for frying

Clean the cardoons and remove any tough stalk end or stringiness. Bring a couple of quarts of water and salt to a boil. Drop in the cardoons. Cook until tender, about 25 minutes. Drain and allow to cool. Slice into 4-inch strips. Beat eggs in a shallow bowl. Place bread crumbs in another shallow bowl. Heat about 1/8-inch layer of oil in a large heavy skillet. Depending on the width of the cardoon stalks, take 3 or 4 at a time with a fork. Dip into egg first, then into bread crumbs and immediately into hot oil. Fry on both sides until golden brown. Add oil to pan as necessary. Place cutlets on double thickness of paper toweling to drain. You can save and reheat any leftover cutlets.

Grace (daughter): Once in grammar school, St. Mary's, I brought a leftover artichoke to school and was eating it while sitting with two friends. After eating a few leaves, one of my friends asked if she could taste some artichoke. I answered, "Sure help yourself." The other girl looked on in amazement and said what are you doing. When we explained how to eat an artichoke she said "Oh! I thought you kept tasting it and didn't like it so you were throwing it out!"

Camille (daughter): I had a similar experience, introducing my date, who was in his early thirties, to his first artichoke. What a deprived childhood he had. We were at a restaurant. He watched closely how I would pluck a leaf and clean the meat off with my bottom teeth. More than half way through the artichoke, I noticed he was putting the leaves upside down in his mouth, not getting any artichoke meat. He never complained or seemed to wonder why I was making such sounds of enjoyment. We had a few more dates after that. I'm not sure he ever ate another 'choke.

Polenta

Note from us: We heard that Thomas Jefferson, who according to our Dad, wanted the newly formed America to have Italian as its official language, was the one who brought polenta to the U.S. and it became a forerunner to grits. We decided this is a fact too good to check.

Yield: Puh-lenty

9 Cups Cold Water
2 Cups Coarse Cornmeal
1 Cup Stone-ground Cornmeal
1 Tablespoon Salt

Put the cold water in a nice big pot with a cover. Stir in both of the cornmeals and mix with a long wooden spoon until the solution is smooth and there are no lumps. Turn on the fire moderately high and cook, constantly stirring. If you don't stir you will end up with lumps. Now, when you see the mixture is about to boil, quickly turn down the flame or else the cornmeal will start going plop plop and spitting at you and it burns, so be careful. You want to keep stirring as the mixture thickens, about 3 minutes from the point it starts to boil and go plop plop. When it's pretty thick turn off the flame and pour the polenta into a well-oiled ovenproof dish. Let it set and then you can slice it and serve as a side dish, or reheat slices as needed.

Vegetarian Hint: you can slice cold pieces of this polenta, put them on a pizza tray, top with tomato sauce and cheeses, bake till hot, and you have, voila, Pizza Polenta. It's delicious.

Special Menus

Meet Michael

Michael is Carmela's grandson (son of Chuck and Cheri). More than ten years ago, after Mike got his art degree from the University of Santa Barbara, he set off for—where else?—adventure in Italy. The lure of the world's finest art might have called Mike. But the lure of something else— the world's finest gastronomy—is what has kept Mike there all these years, making him a naturalized citizen and more. Soon after his arrival in Italy, Mike enrolled in chef school in Bologna. Eventually he began working in fine restaurants in Italy and learning all the secrets of this fantastic cuisine. Along the way Mike met his wife, Anastasia, an émigré also to Italy, from Russia. Today, three bambini later, Mike still cooks with great chefs and for his family. We managed to get Mike to offer a few of the dishes he cooks at home.

Michael's Tart

Mike says, "This recipe Anastasia got when she was translating at an Italian cooking class for a group of Russians. He says that in Italy where they live, they always have chestnut flour on hand in the fall for making a dish called *castagnaccio*, "a super poor man's meal with just chestnut flour and water baked in the oven." How resourceful is that for a big Italian family?

We instantly loved this dessert below, with pears and chestnut flour* and of course chocolate never hurts our kids' feelings. We like it sweet but not too sweet."

Mike offers the recipe in grams, saying "that's how I roll!" Of course nearly the whole world does except for us Americans. We decided to leave his recipe as is, given that these most cooking utensils in the U.S. have measurements in both the metric and British systems. You can also find equivalents online. *Buona fortuna!*

Chestnut Flour, Pear and Chocolate Tart

Yield: 6 Servings

For the tart dough:
500 grams Chestnut flour
400 grams Butter, at room temperature
150 grams Sugar
2 Eggs

For the filling:
350 grams Pears that have been pitted, peeled (peeling is optional)
and sliced thin
200 grams Melted Dark Chocolate

Make the dough by working the butter with the sugar and then mix in
the eggs and finally the chestnut flour. Divide the dough in half. Roll
each half out with a rolling pin, either on a floured surface or between
two pieces of parchment paper. Roll to a little under half an inch thick
covering a ten-inch pie tin. Fill with the pear slices and drizzle over
the melted chocolate. Cover with the other half rolled out dough,
crimp the sides and make some holes with a fork for steam vents.
Cook at 350 degrees for 30 to 40 mins. Serve warm or at room
temperature. A dollop of slightly sweetened whip cream with some
cinnamon in it makes this a regal dessert.

Michael's Eggplant and Mozzarella Lasagna

Says Mike, "This dish is a cross between pasta alla norma and eggplant parmigiana, two Italian classics that are loved world over. It is simply playing on the pleasant marriage of fried eggplant, tomato, cheese, and basil."

Yield: 6 to 8 Servings

4 Sheets Egg Pasta (page 62)
5 Cups Tomato Sauce (page 86)
2 Cups Grated Mozzarella
4 Cups Eggplant, cubed and fried in olive oil
½ Cup Grated Parmigiana
1 Cup Chopped Fresh Basil

Once you have all your ingredients together you can begin to assemble. First layer a sheet of pasta. Then cover some tomato sauce. Next add some eggplant and mozzarella. Sprinkle parmigiana and basil. Begin again with pasta and continue until you finish the ingredients. **IMPORTANT:** Make the last layer the pasta dough covered with sauce and parmigiana. Bake at 350 degrees for 40 to 45 minutes. Let cool slightly and serve.

Michael's Spaghetti with Bottarga and Citrus

No Bottarga?* No worries. Mike offers some substitutes below*
*Here's what he says about this recipe that arouses great nostalgia for
him, a "born-again" Italian: "As a student of art in Bologna when we
would come in late at night (or should I say early in the morning?),
we would always gather in someone's apartment and make spaghetti
aglio olio e pepperoncino. Everyone had their version down to the
details of how to cut and fry the garlic. Every way was delicious, of
course, but I particularly liked the way my friend Roberto Rinaldi
showed me. It is thanks to him that I am a chef today. One day he said
to me, "Mike, you like cooking so much, why don't you go to culinary
school?" The rest is history. Here is my version of Roberto's pasta
with bottarga."*

Yields: 4 to 6 Servings

½ Cup Extra Virgin Olive Oil
3 Cloves Garlic, finely chopped
Dried chili flakes or if you prefer, 2 fresh chili peppers, chopped
2 Tablespoons Water
1 cup coarsely chopped Parsley
Grated zest of 2 Lemons and 2 oranges
1 Pound Spaghetti

Add the oil, garlic, chili flakes (or fresh chilis), and water to a saute
pan, and place over medium heat. When the water has evaporated,
your garlic should have cooked off the raw taste but will not be burnt.
Turn off the heat. Cook the pasta in salted water to your preferred
doneness. When the pasta is ready add it to a large mixing bowl and
toss in the sautéed mixture, parsley and citrus zests. Top individual
servings with grated bottarga (or your chosen substitute, below).

*Bottarga is the Italian name for a delicacy of salted, cured fish roe,
usually from mullet or tuna. If you substitute something else for the
bottarga you will have a different dish, but it will still be delicious.
Mike suggests: "Top the pasta with grilled soft-shell crabs or quality
canned tuna and bread crumbs or even pieces of reconstituted
baccalà."

Meet Tom

Tom, Carmela's youngest son, probably has the best and most extensively equipped kitchen of all the ten kids. His wife, Patty, might agree with him, that he taught her how to cook, although when you go to their home they are usually both in the kitchen, chef and sous-chef (alternating roles). To this day, we all wonder why Tom never opened his own restaurant. Maybe he was too busy raising four kids. And besides, he says, he cooks food for the love of it, not to make a living (or a killing). We managed to get him to share a few of his easy recipes and secrets (like the meatball one. It was not easy to get it written down, because like many who love to cook, he says, "I don't measure when I cook, I go by feel and taste so I will do my best to suggest measurements." All of which is to say, good luck!

Tom's Famous Meatballs

Tom says, "Be careful with this recipe because if you overdo any ingredient it can overpower the taste of the meatball. However, if you add the right amounts mixed with a pinch of love it will be the best tasting meatball you or your family and friends ever had.

Yield: 8 to 12 meatballs

2 Tablespoons Butter
5 to 6 Cloves Garlic, chopped
½ Medium-size Sweet Onion, chopped
1 Pound Lean Ground Beef
1 Cup Ricotta Cheese
1 to 2 Tablespoons A-1 Sauce
1 Tablespoon Worcestershire Sauce
1 Tablespoon Soy Sauce
1 Cup Grated Parmesan Cheese
½ Cup Seasoned Italian Bread Crumbs
1 Egg
3 Tablespoons Chopped Fresh Parsley
2 Tablespoons Olive Oil

(continued)

Melt the butter in a medium-size sauté pan. Add the garlic then the onions. Saute' until very soft, translucent and aromatic. Let cool, then grind the mixture in a small Cuisinart. The mixture should be finely pureed with no lumps or signs of the original onion or garlic.

Place the chopped meat in large mixing bowl. Add the onion and garlic mixture, along with all of the other ingredients except the olive oil. Like the old-time Italians, use your hands to mix all together well.

Form the meat into medium-size meatballs. A pound of meat generally makes between 8 to 12 meatballs. I usually get about 10. My preference is gently fry the meat in olive oil in a saute' pan until brown on all sides and then place in my red sauce. An easier and slightly less messy method, is to place the raw meatballs in a glass baking dish and bake at 375 to 400 degrees for about 20 to 30 minutes until browned.

TOM'S LINGUINE WITH CLAMS & OYSTERS

No doubt you've enjoyed the popular spaghetti with clam sauce—either a red or white one. This is Tom's variation on that theme.

Yield: 4 to 6 Servings

1 Pound Linguine
3 Tablespoons Olive Oil
12 Cloves Garlic (or as much as you can handle), chopped
1 Can White Clam Sauce (Progresso is a good choice)
1 Can Oysters
1 Can Chicken Broth
Salt and Pepper to taste
Chopped Fresh Parsley
Grated Parmesan

While the linguine is cooking, prepare the sauce. Heat the olive oil and stir in the garlic and sauté it until lightly brown and tender. Stir in the clams, oysters, and broth and heat well. Season with salt and pepper to taste. Toss with the cooked linguine. Top each serving with parsley and grated Parmesan.

Tom's Quick & Healthy Pasta Dishes

Tom says, "Most Americans think of pasta as a meal to be had with red sauce but pasta goes with just about any vegetable, fish or meat. The sauce can be based on olive oil, pesto, chicken or beef broth. If you ever have any leftover chicken, sausage, beef, fish. Add to your pasta with some red bell peppers, onions, garlic, mushrooms or any combination of these. Some of my favorite pasta types are: Casarecce, Gemelli, Penne, Ziti, or Rigate. All are sold in bulk at very reasonable prices at Costco. Also note: Most chefs cook pasta with salt added to the water but I don't add any salt, as I feel there is enough is in the ingredients I add to the pasta dish. Which lets me think it is a bit healthier."

Pasta with chicken, mushrooms, and pesto sauce

Yield 3 to 4 Servings

1 Pound Pasta
1 Cup Sliced Mushrooms
2 to 3 Tablespoons Butter
Any leftover baked or cooked chicken, sliced into small thin pieces
Salt and Pepper to taste
2 to 3 Tablespoons Pesto Sauce (store bought or see page 88)
Grated Parmesan Cheese

While the pasta is boiling, sauté the mushrooms in butter. Add salt and pepper to taste. Add the chicken pieces to the sauté pan and allow to heat through. Toss the chicken and mushrooms with the cooked pasta. Add the pesto sauce, toss and serve. Let each diner top the pasta with grated parmesan cheese.

PASTA VARIATIONS: You can replace the chicken with cooked sausage. Or, if you prefer to go meatless, try adding sautéed red bell peppers, asparagus, and mushrooms, to your cooked pasta, seasoned to taste. Drizzle a little pesto or some very good olive oil over the pasta and serve with grated parmesan cheese

Tom's Dates and Bacon Appetizer

Tom says, "This is an appetizer that usually goes over well with our guests. The mix of flavors—tangy Chèvre (or goat) cheese, salty bacon or prosciutto, and sweet date—is very pleasing to most palates."

Dates
Chèvre (goat cheese)
Bacon Slices

Slice each date down the middle and remove the pit if necessary. Stuff the date with some goat cheese. One bacon slice goes a long way, and depending on the size you can usually cut the bacon strip into at least 4 pieces and often as many as 6 slices. The slices should be long enough to wrap around the circumference of the date.

Wrap each cheese-stuffed date with a bacons strip. Make sure it holds together and place on a pizza tin. When you have enough for your party bake at 375 to 400 degrees for about 15 minutes, until the bacon is fairly crisp. Serve warm or at room temperature.

VARIATION: You can replace the bacon with prosciutto but don't bake as long as the prosciutto is much thinner and will cook much faster.

Tom's Fresh Tomatoes with *Burrata* Appetizer

This is one of those deceptively simple preparations whose success relies on the goodness of each ingredient. Use only the best for this appetizer. This is a variation on the Caprese Salad that has grown in popularity in recent years. Burrata, like fresh mozzarella, is made from Buffalo milk but is more delicate, creamier, and subtle than the latter.

Ripe Fresh Tomatoes
Burrata Cheese
Balsamic Vinegar
Extra Virgin Olive Oil
Sprigs of Fresh Basil
Salt and Pepper

Wash your fresh tomatoes, slice, no more than a quarter-inch thick and spread on a serving plate. Slice the Burrata cheese and place pieces on each tomato slice. Drizzle your finest olive oil over each tomatoes. Then, drizzle balsamic vinegar over the tomatoes. Sprigs of fresh basil are best but dried basil is fine too. Add salt and pepper to taste and serve.

Desserts, baked goods, quick breads, cookies

We didn't get a lot of dessert growing up as a big family, although Mom loved to bake. We sometimes had cherry Jell-O or Ice Box Cake (Graham Crackers layered with My-T-Fine chocolate pudding and banana slices). We had a Dugan man who drove a truck, came to the door once in awhile, and talked Mom's ear off (she didn't seem to mind). She would appease him and take a pecan coffee ring or crumb cake to have with our bottomless cup of percolated Yuban coffee. There was a mysterious buttery pound cake, too, that came in a long plain brown box with no marking. It might have originated from the same source as the cans of food with no labels that Dad brought home. When we got a little older Mom was able to bake a lot more often. Born dunkers, we loved her cookies. She briefly had a cake decorating business, Kakes by Kay (her nickname). Mom was the Michelangelo of wedding cakes. She was a veritable sculptor.

Carmela's handcrafted wedding cake for Terry (1964), her first one after taking courses. Many more to come.

159

Cannoli Shells and Filling

These take some time to make but they are worthwhile if you can't find ready-made shells. My brother would say homemade are the best anyway. You can find the cannoli cylinders in most stores wherever Italian cooks are nearby.

Yield: 24 Servings

3 Cups Flour
1/4 Teaspoon Cinnamon
2 Tablespoons Sugar
2 Tablespoons Shortening
3/4 Cup Dry Red Wine
2 Quarts Light Oil For Frying

Mix flour, cinnamon, and sugar. Mix in shortening as you would mix for pie, making a crumbly mixture, then add wine slowly until a ball is formed. Knead the dough just enough to achieve an elastic consistency. Excessive kneading will cause the pastry to become tough. Place dough on a floured cloth and let it rest for 15 minutes. Meanwhile begin to heat the oil to 350 degrees in large pot. After dough has rested, take a piece of dough the size of a walnut and roll in 5-inch circle and wrap around cannoli cylinder and secure end with egg white. Fry for a few minutes till a nice brown color. Remove with a slotted spoon and let cool on many layers of paper towel to absorb excess oil. Don't be dismayed if the first few shells come undone in the oil—just press the dough closing a littler more tightly. Store the shells in a cookie tin in a cool dry place.

Filling:
2 pounds ricotta
1 Tablespoon vanilla
1 almond Hershey bar, grated (small)
1 cup powdered sugar
1/2 pint heavy cream, whipped
Some Chopped Pistachio Nuts (optional)

Mix ricotta, vanilla, grated Hershey, and sugar till smooth. Whip up heavy cream and fold into Ricotta mixture. Fill cannoli shells with a pastry bag only when ready to serve. Dip ends of filled cannoli in chopped pistachio nuts, if desired

Carmela with one of her many wedding cakes

Pizzelle (Italian waffle cookies)

These Italian cookies are easy to make. You can find a pizzelle iron (like a waffle iron but smaller) in most home goods stores now. American style-pizzelle calls for vanilla flavoring. The classic Italian one uses licorice-scented anise. Both are good. These make a nice addition to any holiday cookie tray.

Yield: About 3 dozen *pizzelle*

3 Eggs
1/2 Cup Sugar
1/2 Cup Butter, Melted
1 Teaspoon Ground Anise Seeds
2 Cups Flour
1 1/2 Teaspoons Baking Powder

Beat the eggs and sugar. Mix in the butter. Sift together the anise, flour, and baking powder and stir into the batter until smooth.
Heat the pizzelle iron and brush on some vegetable oil. Pour about a tablespoon of batter on each of the iron circles. Bake for about 30 seconds. You will know after a few tries, how long is best. Remove the crispy cookies, allow to cool. Store the pizzelle in an airtight cookie tin.

Nut and Poppy Seed Rolls (Kolach)

This recipe was one of Mrs. Koye's (Mom's brother's mother-in-law).
She was a good cook.

Yield: 12 Servings

Pastry:
2 Pkgs Yeast,
1/2 Cup Warm Water
7 Cups Flour
1 Cup Sugar
1 Teaspoon Salt
1 Pound Crisco
Evaporated Canned Milk, as needed
6 Eggs

Dissolve yeast in warm water. In large bowl, mix flour, sugar, and salt. Add Crisco and enough milk till crumbly. Add eggs and yeast mixture. Mix together with enough milk to make workable dough. Put into bowl and refrigerate for 3 hours.

While dough chills, make the filling of choice (below).

Remove dough from refrigerator and cut it into 8 pieces. Roll each piece one at a time into 10 x 15-inch rectangle. Spread some filling on the rolled dough.

Roll it up jelly-roll fashion and crimp ends to seal. Place rolls on cookie sheet seam down (4 on each cookie sheet). Before putting in oven make some small slashes across the top and brush the top with some beaten egg. Bake at 350 degrees about 30 minutes or until nice and golden. Remove from oven and place on rack to cool. You can freeze the baked rolls once they are cooled.

Nut filling
2 Pounds Walnuts, Ground Fine
1 1/2 Cups Sugar
Rind of One Lemon, Grated
6 Eggs whites Beaten Stiff

Mix all ingredients together until well blended.

(continued)

Poppy Seed filling:
1 pound Poppy Seeds
1 Cup Milk
Pat of butter
1 1/2 cups sugar
1/2 cup honey
Zest of 1/2 lemon

Cook poppy seeds, milk, and butter together for about 15 minutes. Cool, slightly and add remaining ingredients.

Cranberry Nut Bread

My friend Frances gave me this recipe over the phone. The first time I made it, it was a disaster. I heard 3 cups of sugar instead of 3/4 cup. Well it went in the garbage, but I never give up and will make it again soon. . . She raves about it. Nice to give to friends for the holiday.

Yield: 1 loaf or 18 muffins

1 1/3 Cups Flour
1 Teaspoon Baking Soda
1 1/4 Teaspoons Baking Powder
1/2 Teaspoon Salt
3/4 Cup Sugar
Peel From 1 orange
6 Tablespoon Butter, Cut Into 1-Inch Pieces
1 Teaspoon Lemon Juice
2 Large Eggs
1/4 Cup Fresh Orange Juice
1 1/4 Cups Fresh Cranberries
1 Cup Walnuts

Preheat oven to 350 degrees. Combine flour, baking soda, baking powder and salt in bowl. Stir to mix; set aside. With metal blade in place, add sugar and orange peel to bowl of food processor. Process until the peel is finely chopped. Add butter and lemon juice. Turn on and off rapidly until combined. Add eggs and orange juice; process until smooth. Add cranberries and nuts. Turn on and off 5 or 6 times. Add flour mixture and turn off only until flour disappears, about 3 or 4 pulses. Turn into a well greased 9 x 5 x 3-inch loaf pan or 18 paper lined 2-3/4-inch muffin cups. Bake 1 hour for the loaf and 30 minutes for the muffins. Remove from pan and cool on wire rack.

Cranberry Scones

I found this recipe in a magazine. The scones are made in star shape and made for Christmas, but I like scones any time so why wait for Christmas to make. I find these tastier than other scones I have had. Serve scones warm. If you do not have star cookie cutter, cut in triangles. The taste is what counts.

Yield: 6 Servings

1 Teaspoon Ground Cinnamon
1/4 Cup + 1 Tablespoon Sugar
1 1/2 Cups Flour
1 1/4 Teaspoon Baking Powder
1 Teaspoon Salt
1/2cup Margarine or 1 Stick Butter
1/2 Cup Dried Cranberries or 1 Tablespoon Sugar-Raisins
1/4 Cup Sour Cream
1/4 Cup Orange Juice
2 Teaspoons Orange Peel

Preheat oven to 400 degrees. Grease large cookie sheet. In cup, with fork, mix cinnamon and 1 tablespoon sugar; set aside. In medium bowl, mix flour, baking powder, salt, and 1/4 cup sugar. With pastry blender or two knives used scissor-fashion, cut in margarine or butter until mixture resembles coarse crumbs. Stir in dried cranberries, sour cream, orange juice, and orange peel just until ingredients are blended. Turn dough onto lightly floured surface; with floured rolling pin, lightly roll dough to 1/2-inch thickness. Cut out scones with 3-inch star-shape cookie cutter. With spatula, place scones 2 inches apart on cookie sheet. Press trimmings together; roll and cut as above. Sprinkle scones with cinnamon mixture. Bake scones 10 to 12 minutes until golden.

Pumpkin Bread

This is an easy recipe to make for Thanksgiving or any time. It is very moist. Aunt Lily gave me this recipe many years ago. The recipe was given to me without a method of putting together, but I mixed everything together and it worked fine, so here it is.

Yield: 20 Servings

4 Eggs
2 1/2 Cups Sugar
1/2 Teaspoon Baking Powder
2 Teaspoons Baking Soda
1 1/2 Teaspoons Salt
1 Teaspoon Nutmeg
1 Teaspoon Cinnamon
2 Teaspoons Ground Cloves
3 1/2 Cups Flour
2/3 Cups Water
1 Cup Vegetable Oil
15 Ounce Can Pumpkin
1 Cup Nuts, Chopped

Beat the eggs. Add the sugar and continue beating. In a small bowl, mix baking powder, baking soda, salt, nutmeg, cinnamon, and cloves. Add to flour. Add water and vegetable oil to eggs and sugar and mix well. Then combine flour mixture, pumpkin and nuts. Pour into 2 greased loaf pans. Bake at 350 degrees for 1 hour or until breads test done—a toothpick comes out clean.

Terry (oldest daughter):   Among my memorable times of me and Mom cooking in the kitchen are the times when we were a lot poorer with our father working several jobs to keep the family fed and in clothes. One of Dad's jobs was in the newly opened supermarket in our home town as the night manager. He would bring home dented and unlabeled cans of food, which we placed on a rack at the bottom of our cellar steps. We never knew what the cans contained as we shook them and tried to guess. Was it a can of Le Sueur peas, dog food, Campbell's soup, or a gourmet something or other? One Thanksgiving Mom and I opened up what looked like a can of pumpkin, which we saved to make pumpkin pie for the large number of company we would have at our Thanksgiving feast. Mom and I agreed it was the best pumpkin pie we ever tasted but thought for many years that it had to be something other than pumpkin but we would never know.

Grace (daughter): Another *sweet* memory was visiting Mom with my friend Laurie to make baklava. Laurie was a chef and loved talking with Mom about baking and cooking. Sadly, Laurie died too young, on November 14, 2006. But I wonder if they're up there together, Mom and Laurie, talking food and enjoying wine! Laurie loved her wine, too!

Apple Coffee Cake

This recipe was given to me by my friend Frances Gadomski. It was handed down to her by her mother.

Yield: 12 Servings

2 Cups Plus 5 Tablespoons Sugar
5 Large Apples, Chopped
5 Teaspoons Cinnamon
3 Cups Flour
2 Teaspoons Baking Powder
1 Teaspoon Salt
1 Cup Salad Oil
4 Large Eggs
1/4 Cup Orange Juice
1 Teaspoon Vanilla Extract

Combine 5 tablespoons sugar and apples and cinnamon. Mix flour, 2 cups sugar, baking powder, and salt. Make a well in center of flour mixture, pour in oil, eggs, orange juice and vanilla. Blend well. Spoon 1/3 mixture into greased tube pan. Place half the apples on mixture making sure that the apples do not touch the side of the pan. Spoon another 1/3 batter on apples. Place the rest of apples on top of remaining batter. Bake approximately 1 1/4 hours. Cover with foil if cake is getting two brown. Bake at 350 degrees.

Sponge Cake

I like sponge cakes, because they are light and great tasting, especially with custard.

Yield: 15 Servings

6 Large Eggs, Separated
1 Teaspoon Vanilla Extract
1 Cup Sugar, divided
1/2 Cup All Purpose Flour
1/2 Cup Corn Starch
Pinch Salt

Butter and line with parchment paper a 9 to 10-inch round cake pan that is 2 inches deep. In a medium mixing bowl, whisk the egg yolks with the vanilla. Whisk in half the sugar and continue to beat until very light and frothy, about 5 minutes, either by hand, with hand mixer set at medium speed, or in a heavy-duty mixer fitted with the whip.

Combine the flour and cornstarch and sift once to aerate. In a clean, dry bowl, beat the egg whites with the salt until they hold a very soft peak, either by hand with a hand mixer set at medium speed, or in a heavy-duty mixer fitted with the whip. Beating faster, add the remaining sugar in a very slow stream, beating until the egg whites hold a firm peak.

Fold the yolk mixture into the whites with a rubber spatula. Sift the flour and cornstarch over the egg in 3 additions, folding them in gradually. Do not over mix the batter.

Pour the batter into the prepared pan and smooth the top. Bake at 350 degrees, for 30 to 40 minutes, until it is well risen and feels firm when pressed gently.

Immediately loosen the layer from the side of the pan with a small knife or spatula. Invert the layer onto a rack and leave the paper stuck to it. Turn the layer right side up and cool it on a rack.

Terry (daughter): When I was getting married in 1964, Mom took cake decorating lessons because she was preparing to finesse her God-given decorating ability to make my wedding cake, which was to be her first of many. I remember she secluded herself in the cellar, which housed a complete kitchen with a second fridge, oven, and baking equipment. It was the day before the wedding was to take place. She spent the whole day down there quietly and uninterrupted putting the cake together. It was beautiful and fed 220 people! Now I wonder if back then she was also in need of that solitude as she might have been contemplating what it would be like for her first daughter to be married and leave the nest. Or *did* I leave the nest?

Chuck (son): Cheri and I were just getting married and starting out with not much. We could not spend much on a wedding. Mom made our wedding cake too.

Lisa (daughter): Yes, mom made my wedding cake as well. I have pictures too. Mom and Dad were living in Dallas at the time of my wedding. Mom packed all of her decorating equipment in their Lincoln Continental and drove to Virginia. I don't know how, but she miraculously made the cakes and decorated them the day before our wedding in the small town home that Vadj (my husband-to-be) was living in. We then moved the decorated tiers to our neighbor's home until the morning of the wedding because so many of the guests were coming to our townhouse. The next day, my wedding day, Mom and Dad drove my very small Subaru with the multi-tiered wedding cake to Arlington to set up at our reception hall. My wedding day was June 24. If you have ever been in the Washington, DC area the week before the Fourth of July, you know traffic is horrendous! How they made it to Arlington and back I will never know!

Tina (daughter): Mom made my wedding cake, too while they were living in Texas. Jody and I got married in Bethlehem. So, yet again Mom, ever at the ready, packed up all of her baking equipment and truck it on over Pennsylvania. After my two youngest, Alexandria and Jesse, were born, I told them stories about Mom making cakes for all different occasions. Mom always sliced off the top of the cakes and put those "scrapings" aside for the family. The customer got a nice-looking cake but we felt lucky because she would make a delicious dessert from the cake trimmings. She layered those scraps with leftover fillings. She was making English trifles before they became popular in this country.

Tom (son): These stories about wedding cakes and Mom always working miracles brought back a memory of her cake making/decorating days. I cannot remember the year but we were still living in Rahway, New Jersey. So it was maybe 1968-69 and we had the Chrysler station wagon that we all used to pile into at times. I would sometimes help Mom and Dad with delivery of some of the wedding cakes.

It was July and Mom was asked to make a multi-tiered wedding cake using sponge cake. Many of you may know it
has a real aerated structure to it and it is not as firm as simple pound cake. It was an exceptionally hot July and Mom put the cake together with all its tiers at the wedding hall. Despite the air-conditioned hall, the combination of the heat and lack of structure of the cake caused the cake to sag downwards. The bottom tiers could not support the top layers.

Mom was really nervous. I never saw her cry like this over a decorated cake as her desperation became overwhelming. This cake was for a young woman's wedding and she was counting on Mom. I have to say that I also remember Dad, who could get easily irritated, in an extremely supporting role on this particular day. He convinced Mom it could be corrected.

Apple Cobbler

Yield: 16 Servings

4 Cups Flour
1 Pound Margarine or Butter
1 Cup Sugar
1 Large Egg
1/2 Cup Coconut
1 Teaspoon Vanilla
2 Jars or Cans Applesauce or any Pie Fruit Filling

Mix flour and margarine or butter and sugar. Mix till flour resembles small peas. Add large egg and coconut, and vanilla. Mix well till all is incorporated. The dough will be on soft side. Divide dough, one piece a little more than half for the bottom. Spray pan (10 X 13) with Pam and coat with a little flour. Press the dough on pan with floured fingers or a rolling pin if you have one that fits in pan. Spread the two cans of applesauce or pie-filling fruit as desired over the bottom dough. With the other portion of dough, take small pieces of dough add over fruit and try to cover dough with little pieces of dough. You will see when baked, it will look like crumbs. Bake for 1 hour or till nicely browned on top. Bake at 375 degrees. When completely baked cool, then sprinkle confectionery sugar on top. Cut in squares when serving. Goes nicely with ice cream.

Donna (daughter): Mom always had a solution for what seemed like the impossible. One time, when I was a teenager, she had an order for a seven-tiered wedding cake for one of her customers. She spent days baking and decorating. On the day of the wedding, three tiers sat on our dining room table; the rest of the tiers were placed carefully next to the first four, ready for assembly after delivery. She had asked to me to vacuum earlier in the day and as a rebellious teenager, I was mad that I had this chore to do. I began angrily pushing the hoover across the floor, the chord flying through the air. I made dramatic movements, picking the sweeper and letting it bang on the floor. Suddenly the chord, channeling my agitation, swept right across the three tiers, destroying two of the beautifully decorated layers. I froze in fear. I knew what a stickler Mom was. I was ready to flee, but instead, in tears, I confessed what happened. When she saw the destruction, she didn't say a word, but got her box of decorating tools and went to work. Within no time, she restored the cake to its former beauty. I was so happy and impressed (and lucky) that she could truly work miracles.

Cassata Cake (Sicilian Cream Cake)

This a delicious cake. It takes some time, but is worth it. I made this cake for Daddy on his birthday. If you think there is too much liquor, you may cut down according to taste.

Yield: 2 8-inch cakes, 12 Servings

1/2 Cup Sugar
1/4 Cup Cornstarch
1/8 Teaspoon Salt
2 1/2 Cups Milk
2 Large Eggs, Slightly Beaten
4 Tablespoons Cream De Cacao
4 Tablespoons Rum
Some cocoa
1 Teaspoon Vanilla
Two 8-inch sponge cakes (see Sponge Cake, page 170)
4 Tablespoons Marsala Wine
1 Pound Ricotta Cheese
1/2 Cup Powdered Sugar
1/2 Pint Heavy Cream, whipped

Combine sugar, cornstarch, and salt on top of double boiler. Add 1/2 cup milk and stir until smooth. Add the remainder of milk and cook over hot water until thick and smooth, stirring constantly. Pour small amount of hot mixture into slightly beaten eggs and return to double boiler. Cook 5 minutes more, until thickened. Put custard in bowl and cover with plastic wrap and cool.

Divide custard in three portions. Add one tablespoon of rum to one part of custard. Make the second custard with enough cocoa and 1/2 teaspoon of vanilla to make it chocolate-y. To the last custard add 1 tablespoon rum.

Cut each cake layer in half through the middle to fill. Put first layer on serving platter. Drizzle some of the remaining liquor and Marsala on each layer of cake before spreading on the custard. You will have three fillings between four layers of sponge cake. *(continued)*

Whip ricotta cheese till smooth. Add powdered sugar. Whip the Cream in another bowl. Add remaining vanilla and fold whipped cream into ricotta and adjust for sweetness. This you spread on sides and top of cake. I also chop some nuts, fine and put on the side of the cake.

Variation: Dash of cinnamon and dash of orange flavor may be added to ricotta.

Jim (firstborn): There is a high level of entrepreneurial energy in our family. Some of it comes from growing up with not many financial resources. Problems always had to be solved positively and creatively. These are two attributes that Mom had in spades—until her dying day. As we all know well, she was an outstanding cake decorator and could have developed it into a major business if she had the financial support and time.

Another one of her early businesses in which I was involved came about when I was 10 years old and we didn't have the financial wherewithal to make ends meet (we were only up to seven kids then). Mom decided to commandeer her mother's old ovens that were sitting unused in the cellar of the two-family home where we lived (on Van Buren Avenue in Elizabeth, N.J.), and use them to create a pizza business. We lived in the downstairs flat and our grandmother (Catalano), who owned the home, lived upstairs.

Since Mom was known in the neighborhood as a great Italian cook, the business took off simply by word-of-mouth. My sister, Terry, helped bake the pizza pies and my father and I delivered them. The problem was that Dad was too charismatic and while making deliveries, he and I were often invited in for a drink and sometimes we even shared in the pizza! Mom was constantly telling him to return home ASAP. But more often than not, she had to reheat the pizzas because he enjoyed customer discussions and of course, a drink here and there.

This adventure taught me a few things at a tender age. If you do what you are good at and love to do and connect it with a need out there, you can succeed. I also learned that any of the entrepreneurial genes in our family came from Mom. Dad was not a big risk taker in the business area He valued the security of his civil service job at the post office. With a minimal amount of funding, Mom in the kitchen, Dad as the front man, and my brothers, sisters and I as waiters, waitresses and kitchen help, we could have had an exciting Italian Restaurant business. But that's a whole other story!

We don't know what Dad was cooking up in this photo taken in New Guinea where he was in the Army Air Corps during World War II (while Carmela was home pregnant with their firstborn). But we suspect he's already planning to do something remarkable, oh, maybe like produce a big family.

Favorite Cheese Cake

I like this cheese cake recipe because it requires no bottom crust and it isn't as rich as some cheese cakes. This is a matter of taste.

Yield: 12 Servings

1 Pound Ricotta Cheese
1 Pound Cream Cheese
1 1/2 Cups Sugar
4 Large Eggs
4 Ounces Butter, Melted
3 Tablespoons Flour
3 Tablespoons Cornstarch
4 Teaspoons Vanilla
Juice of One Lemon
1 Pound Sour Cream

In mixer put ricotta cheese, cream cheese, and sugar. Mix well, then add eggs one at a time mixing well after each addition. Add melted butter and flour and cornstarch, vanilla and lemon juice. Fold in sour cream, making sure all is incorporated and smooth. Pour into greased and floured spring form pan. Bake at 350 degrees for 1 hour. Turn the oven off and then leave cake in the oven for another hour. Remove cake to a rack to cool. Put in refrigerator till ready to serve. Pie filling may be added on top.

Donna (daughter): I just remembered when Mrs. Pindolfo, the really "rich" lady who lived in Ringtown (with the built-in swimming pool) wanted Mommy to teach her how to make Mom's ricotta cheesecake. Mrs. P. kept trying and just couldn't get it right. She kept bringing them over to our home for us to test. Who knows what she was doing, but they were awful. We kept throwing them away and dreading her next attempt. I think Mom convinced her to take up crocheting instead. Hee, hee, It's not for everyone. Although I'm sure the recipe for it in this book will work just fine. If not, take up crocheting.

Hungarian Coffee Cake

This a very popular coffee cake and delicious. It's sometimes called differently, but still the same. My friend gave me this recipe many years ago, and sadly to say, she has passed away. The cake lives on.

Yield: 12 Servings

1/2 Pound Margarine or Butter
2 Cups Sugar
4 Eggs, Separated
1 Pint Sour Cream
4 Teaspoons Vanilla
4 Cups Cake Flour
2 Teaspoons Baking Powder
2 Teaspoons Baking Soda
1/2 Teaspoon salt

Filling:
1 Tablespoon Flour
1/2 Cup Light Brown Sugar
1 Tablespoon Soft Butter or Margarine
1/2 Cup Chopped Walnuts
1 Teaspoon Cinnamon
1 Teaspoon Nutmeg

In bowl, cream butter or margarine thoroughly, gradually add the sugar, beating until light and fluffy. Add the egg yolks, beating well. Add the sour cream and vanilla. Gradually add the sifted and combined flour, baking powder, and soda and salt. Beat the egg whites until stiff. Fold into the batter with a cut-and-fold motion.
Filling: In a bowl combine the flour, brown sugar, soft butter, walnuts, cinnamon, and nutmeg. Mix well, Pour half the batter into a lightly greased and floured 10-inch tube pan. Sprinkle half the filling over batter and top with remaining batter. Sprinkle remaining crumb mixture over top of batter. Bake in 350 degrees oven until golden brown or when toothpick inserted in cake comes away clean. Remove to rack to cool.

Sour Cream Pound Cake

Yield: 12 Servings

3 Cups Sugar
2 Sticks Margarine or Butter
6 Eggs Separated
3 Cups Flour
1/4 Teaspoon Baking Soda
1 Cup Sour Cream
3 Teaspoons Flavoring--Butter or Vanilla

Preheat oven to 350 degrees. Cream sugar and margarine until creamy, add egg yolks, one at time, beating well. Sift flour three times, add soda to sour cream, stir well. Add flour and sour cream alternately to margarine sugar. Blend well, add flavors. Beat egg whites stiff fold into mixture. Bake in tube pan 1 1/2 hours , or until done.

Orange Pineapple Cake
This is very simple and easy to make and makes a big show.

Yield: 12 Servings

1 Box Yellow Cake Mix
1 Can 11-ounce Mandarin Oranges with Juice
4 Large Eggs
1/2 Cup Oil
Frosting:
10 Ounce Can Crushed Pineapple with Juice
1 Small Package Vanilla Instant Pudding
8 Ounce Container Cool Whip

Combine cake mix, oranges with juice, eggs, and oil with electric mixer until oranges are broken up and batter is fluffy (about 3 minutes). Pour into 3 9-inch pans that have been greased and floured. Bake 350 degrees for 20 minutes. Cool on rack before frosting.
Frosting: Mix well the crushed pineapple with juice with the vanilla pudding. Then fold in the cool whip. Frost between the three layers and top and sides of cake. Refrigerate for at least 1 hour before serving.

Prune Sheet Cake

This recipe was given to me by Mom Koye. She had some very good Hungarian recipes.

Yield: 15 Servings

3 Cups Flour, All Purpose
1/4 Cup Sugar
2 Teaspoons Baking Powder
1/2 Pound Butter or Margarine
4 Large Egg Yolks
Canned Milk, Enough To Make Soft Dough
1 1/2 Pounds Prune Butter, or Lekvar (same thing)
4 Large Egg Whites
1/4 Cup Sugar
1 Cup Ground Nuts
1 Teaspoon Lemon Rind

In large bowl put flour with 1/4 cup of sugar and baking powder. Cut in butter till well blended, then add egg yolks and enough canned milk to make a soft dough, that you can handle. Spread dough in a 10 X 13 inch pan. Spread jar of prune butter on dough. Beat 4 egg whites stiff adding second 1/4 cup sugar, nuts, and lemon rind. Spread egg whites mixture over prune butter. Bake 375 degrees for 25 to 30 minutes or when nicely brown.

Ricotta Cake

This recipe was given to me by a friend. It's another way to make Italian cheese cake. It may be dry but that's how it's supposed to be.

Yield: 12 Servings

Crust:
8 Graham Crackers
2 Tablespoons Sugar
5 Tablespoons Melted Butter
Filling:
3 Pounds Ricotta Cheese
1 Cup Sugar
3/4 Cup Bread Crumbs, Plain
6 Large Eggs
1/2 Bag Chocolate Chips, Small Bag
10 Ounce Cherries, Drained
Dash Cinnamon
Pinch Salt

Crust: Take 8 Graham crackers and crumble or grind them. Mix with 2 tablespoons sugar and 5 tablespoons melted butter. Save some of the crumb mix for the top. Press the rest of the crumb mix firmly into bottom and sides of 9-inch spring-form pan. Bake until fragrant and browned around the edges, 12 to 14 minutes. Cool completely.
Mix all the filling ingredients well and pour into the cooled crust. Sprinkle top with some graham crackers. Bake 300 degrees for 1 hour, or until firm. Leave in oven until cold. Leave oven door open about 1 hour till cake is cool. Refrigerate over night.

Strawberry Cream Cake

This a new cake found in McCall's recipe book. It's another way to make a sponge. This was made in 10-inch tube pan. It was split in 3 layers and filled with cream and strawberries.

Yield: 12 Servings

6 Egg Whites
1 3/4 Cups Sifted Flour
1/2 Teaspoon Salt
1 1/2 Cups Granulated Sugar
6 Egg Yolks, Slightly Beaten
1/4 Cup Lemon Juice
2 Tablespoons Water
1 Tablespoon Lemon Peel
Cream and Strawberries

In large mixing bowl, let egg whites warm to room temperature, about 1 hour. Sift flour with salt. With mixer at high speed, beat egg whites until foamy. Beat in 3/4 cup of the granulated sugar, 2 tablespoons at a time, beating after each addition. Beat until soft peaks form when beater is slowly raised.
Preheat oven to 350 degrees.
In small mixing bowl, at high speed and with the same beater, beat yolks until very thick and lemon-colored. Gradually beat in remaining sugar. Beat 2 minutes at low speed, gradually beat in flour mixture. Add lemon juice, 2 tablespoons water and lemon peel, beating just to combine--1 minute. With wire whisk using an under and over motion, gently fold egg-yolk mixture into egg whites just to blend. Pour batter into an ungreased 10-by-4 inch tube pan, bake 40 minutes, or until top springs back when gently pressed with fingertip. Invert pan over neck of a bottle; let cake cool completely about 1 hour. With spatula carefully loosen cake from pan; remove cake. Spread with cream and strawberries.

Tiramisu

This "pick-me-up" cake has been made with different methods. Some may use lady fingers for sponge cake. This is our version.

Yield: 10 Servings

4 Large Eggs
3/4 Cup Sugar
1 Teaspoon Vanilla
3/4 Cup Flour, All Purpose
1/4 Teaspoon Salt
Filling:
1 Pound Mascarpone Cheese
1 Tablespoon Sugar
1 1/2 Cups Whipping Cream
1/4 Cup Brandy
1/4 Cup Sugar
Syrup:
1/2 Cup Boiling Water
1 Tablespoon Instant Espresso Powder
1/4 Cup Brandy
1 Tablespoon Sugar
Cocoa for garnish (optional)

Sponge Cake: Preheat oven to 350 degrees. Grease 15 X 10 X 1-inch jelly roll pan. Line with wax paper; grease and flour paper. Beat eggs in mixer bowl until blended. Gradually add sugar; beat until tripled in volume and batter forms ribbons when beaters are lifted, 10 minutes. Beat in vanilla. Combine flour and salt. Sift unto egg mixture; gently fold in until just blended. Spread into prepared pan. Bake 12 to 15 minutes, until top so cake springs back when lightly touched. Cool in pan on wire rack. Remove wax paper. Cake can be made ahead. Set aside up to 24 hours.

Filling: Stir Mascarpone with sugar in bowl until smooth. Beat cream in mixer bowl till stiff peaks form. Cover and refrigerate 1 cup of beaten cream for decoration; fold remaining cream into mascarpone. *(continued)*

Syrup: Combine all the ingredients in bowl except for the cocoa.

189

Assemble the cake: Cut cake into two 10 X 7 ½-inch rectangles. Trim each half to fit oval or rectangular shallow 2-quart glass dish. Place one layer on bottom and drizzle with 1/2 cup syrup. Spoon on half the filling. Place remaining cake layer on top. Drizzle with 1/2 cup syrup; top with remaining filling. Garnish top with reserved cream. Sift cocoa over top of cake. Cover and refrigerate 4 to 24 hours before serving with reserved cream.

Note: 8 ounces of cream cheese with 1/2 cup of sour cream may be used in place of Mascarpone cheese.
Grace says you can replace the Brandy with Kahlua. And if you want to go totally non-alcoholic she uses Hershey Syrup.

Grace (daughter): For many years while Mom and Dad were living in Maryland I would go down a few weeks before Christmas to bake cookies. We would always make sesame and pignoli cookies. She loved the efficiency of the two-person operation. Many years ago she gave me the recipe for biscotti. After writing the ingredients, her instructions were to bake, brown and pile high. I didn't understood what she meant by "pile high" and when I asked her about it, neither did she! We both had a good laugh about it! I still have the recipe card. Some things you just can't let go!

Biscotti (Twice Baked or Sliced Cookies)

This recipe was given to me by a friend. I make them often, because they are simple and go fast. I like to have a supply of these all the time. They are great with coffee whether you dunk or not.

Yield: 70 Servings

1/2 Pounds Margarine or Butter
1 1/2 Cups Sugar
5 Large Eggs
1 Teaspoon Lemon Flavor
1 Teaspoon Anisette or 1/4 Teaspoon Anise Oil
4 Cups Flour
1/4 Teaspoon Salt
3 Teaspoons Baking Powder
1 Large Egg With 2 Tablespoons Milk for Egg Wash

In a bowl with an electric mixer cream margarine or butter, beat in sugar a little at a time, till mixture is light and fluffy. Add 5 large eggs one at a time, beating well after each addition. Add lemon and Anisette flavors. Sift flour, salt and baking powder. Add to egg mixture. If too sticky add flour enough to handle. Put dough on bread board and divide the dough into 8 rolls. Roll each piece to about 12 inches long. Lay 4 rolls each on two greased cookie sheets. Paint with egg wash. Bake in the upper third of preheated oven 375 degrees for 20 to 25 minutes or till golden brown. Put on board and cool slightly. Cut slices diagonally into ¾-inch slices. Lay cookies on side in pan and toast for about 5 to 10 minutes.

Ricotta Cookies

Yield: A Bunch

1/2 Pound Margarine
2 Cups Sugar
3 Large Eggs
1 Pound Ricotta
1 Teaspoon Salt
1 Teaspoon Baking Powder
4 Cups Flour

Icing:
A Few Drops Milk
2 Cups Powdered Sugar
A Few Drops Vanilla or Lemon flavoring
Sprinkles, optional

Beat margarine and sugar. Add eggs one at a time, then add the remaining ingredients up to the flour. Drop cookies on a greased sheet by the teaspoonful. Bake at 350 for 12 minutes or when the edges start to turn brown. Remove the cookies from the oven.
Make icing: Add the Drops of milk and flavoring to the sugar to make a soft icing but too runny. Dip the cookies in the icing then sprinkle them if desired.

Fancy Cookies

Yield: A bunch

1 Pound Unsalted Butter
1 1/2 Cup Extra Fine Sugar
5 Large Eggs
1 Teaspoon Vanilla
4 or 5 Cups Flour
5 Teaspoons Baking Powder
1 Cup Chopped Nuts

Cream butter and sugar, Add eggs one at a time. Mix 4 cups of flour and baking powder. Add to egg mixture, add vanilla. Add nuts, add more flour if needed to make a soft dough. Refrigerate for an 1 hour. Take small amount of dough, roll in a rope, 1 inch in diameter. Then cut each cookie to size of finger. Bake on an ungreased cookie sheet at 350 degrees for 15 to 20 minutes, till lightly brown. When cool you can decorate the cookies by dipping in melted chocolate and then dip in sprinkles or chopped nuts. Also, you may leave them plain and sprinkle with powder sugar. Delicious.

Fig Cookies (*cucidati*)

These cookies are usually made for Christmas. Sometimes called Christmas cookies. There are different recipes, but this my version.

Yield: A bunch

Dough:
8 Cups Sifted Flour
1 Cup Sugar
3 Tablespoons Baking Powder
1/4 Teaspoon Salt
1 1/2 Cups Shortening
3 Large Eggs
1 Cup Milk, Approximately
1 1/2 Teaspoons Vanilla Extract
1 1/2 Teaspoons Anise Flavoring
Filling:
1 pound figs
1 pound roasted almond or other nuts
1/2 cup honey
zest of one orange and juice
1 Teaspoon cinnamon
1 Teaspoon all spice
1 Tablespoon each brandy, orange liqueur or any on hand.

Sift flour, measure, and resift with sugar, baking powder, and salt. Cut in shortening with fingers until mixture resembles corn meal. Make a well in flour, and break eggs into it. Add half of the milk, and both flavorings. I like to mix the dough in processor. It is much easier. Knead well for 5 minutes, adding the balance of the milk gradually as you knead. Add only enough milk to make a medium soft dough that is easy to handle. Make the filling: Mix all ingredients in food processor or whatever is convenient. *(continued)*

Take some dough and roll it to about 1/8 inch thickness, maybe 10 X 10 inches, give or take. Spoon some fig filling along the top edge and roll the dough over to cover the filling. Cut along the edge so it is sealed. Cut the filled dough in 1-inch pieces and with a sharp knife, make a slit on the side. Continue with the rest of the dough and fig mixture. Lay the cookies on a sheet and paint with egg white. Bake at 350 degrees for 20 minutes or until lightly brown. You can put sprinkles on or ice after baked.

Coconut Cookies

These were given to me by a cousin, Rosalie, who loved to cook. They make quite a bit. You might want to cut the recipe in half. Or quarters.

Yield: A bunch

6 Large Eggs
2 Cups Orange Juice
8 Ounces Coconut
1 Cup Milk
1 Pound Margarine or Butter
4 Pounds Flour
2 Cups Sugar
12 Teaspoons Baking Powder,

Mix all ingredients well. Drop by teaspoons on greased cookie sheet. Bake at 350 degrees until lightly toasted. Make an icing of powdered sugar and milk or orange juice thin enough to coat cookies.

Filbert Nut Cookies *(Quaresimali)*

These cookies are named for the 40 days of Lent and because fats were not eaten then, you will find that these cookies haven't any shortening. They are very hard, but delicious. Usually eaten with either coffee or wine. Don't be afraid to dunk.

Yield: 70 Servings

1 1/2 Pounds Filberts
4 Cups Flour
1 Cup Confectionery Sugar
1 1/2 Cups Brown Sugar
2 Teaspoons Cinnamon
1 Teaspoon Baking Powder
1 Teaspoon Baking Soda
4 Large Eggs
2 Tablespoons Honey
1 Large Egg, mixed With 1 Tablespoon of Water to Baste

Toast filberts on a cookie sheet about 10 minutes at 350 degrees. When toasted, put in dish towel and roll around trying to get the inner skins off as much as possible. Chop in processor coarsely, not too fine. In mixer put all dry ingredients except nuts. Beat the 4 eggs slightly and add to dry ingredients. Add the honey. Mix well. Add filberts to mix. Add some flour only if needed. Try not to use much flour. If dough is hard to handle, oil hands. This makes it easier to handle dough. Put on bread board and cut dough into 4 loaves about 15 X 3 inches. Put on greased baking sheet 3 inches apart. Beat 1 egg with water and paint loves. Bake at 375 degrees for 20 to 25 minutes in the upper third of the oven. Remove to board and slice on diagonal 3/4 inch. Put back in oven and toast cookies on their sides for 15 minutes. Enjoy.

Hungarian Cookies

This was given to me by Mrs. Koye. She was a good baker, but sometimes hard to get the exact recipe. This is pretty good as I worked it out.

Yield: A bunch

1/2 Cup Milk
2 Package Yeast
6 Cups Flour
1/2 Teaspoon Salt
1/2 Cup Sugar
1 Pounds Crisco or Butter
6 Large Eggs, Separated
1 Pint Sour Cream
2 Teaspoons Vanilla or Lemon Flavor
2 Cups Ground Walnuts
1 Cup Sugar

Warm the milk to dissolve yeast and set mixture aside. In bowl put flour, salt and 1/2 cup sugar. Add shortening and mix well. Make a hole and add egg yolks, sour cream, milk, yeast mixture, and vanilla or lemon flavor. Mix well. Add flour if too wet, add milk if too dry. Work it till you have a soft dough, but not sticky. Refrigerate over night.
Filling: Beat egg whites until stiff. Add 1 cup of sugar and ground walnuts. To assemble, take a piece of dough, and roll in about 5 inches in diameter. Cut in 8 pieces like a pie and fill each segment with nut filling. Roll up like a crescent roll. Bake at 350 degrees about 20 minutes or till lightly brown.

Italian Machine Cookies or Cookie Cutter

I call these machine cookies. I make them with our sausage grinder. My cousin made a die that fits the sausage grinder, I put the dough in the top and turn the handle. The cookies come out with a design. They also can be made with cookie cutter.

Yield: A bunch

8 Cups Flour
2 1/2 Cups Sugar
3 Tablespoons Baking Powder
7 Eggs
1/2 Cup Butter, Melted
1/2 Cup Shortening
1 Tablespoon Vanilla
1/2 Ounce Whiskey or Brandy

In a very large bowl, mix the flour, sugar, and baking powder. Make a hole in the middle and add the eggs, melted butter, shortening, vanilla, and whiskey. Start mixing by stirring the eggs and flavorings in middle and bringing the flour in the middle until all is incorporated and you have workable dough. At this point I separate the dough in two. If you find this very hard, I would suggest to start with 1/2 recipe. Bake at 350 degrees, about 15 minutes, or until done. Everyone seems to like these cookies. They go nicely with coffee or a drink.

Pastichioti

An Italian recipe for a pastry. Maybe you can use the 12 leftover egg whites to make a yolk-less omelet.

Yield: 12 Cakes

Pastry:
6 Cups Flour
2 1/2 Cups Sugar
3 Teaspoons Baking Powder
2 Cups Crisco
6 Egg Yolks, Unbeaten
4 1/2 Teaspoons Vanilla
1/8 Cup Milk
Filling:
1 Pound Ricotta
1 1/2 Cups Sugar
6 Egg Yolks
1/4 Cup Milk
1 1/2 Teaspoons Orange Extract
1 1/2 Teaspoons Vanilla

Pastry: Mix flour, sugar, and baking powder. Cut in Crisco until well blended and dough is size of small peas. Make a well in middle of flour. Add 6 egg yolks, vanilla, and milk. Mix well. Roll dough about 1/8-inch thick. Cut round circles large enough to fit in muffin pans. Fill with ricotta mixture.

Filling: Blend ricotta and sugar until well blended. Add 6 egg yolks one at a time and mix well. Add remaining ingredients. Fill muffins with ricotta mixture and then cover with a small piece of dough and seal. Bake for 20 minutes at 350 degrees for 25 minutes.

Pecan Butter Balls

These are similar to Russian cookies. Grace gave me this recipe for (my granddaughter) Patty's Wedding since I made a large tray of assorted cookies. These were a hit.

Yield: 50

2 Cups Finely Chopped Pecans
2 Teaspoons Vanilla
2 Cups Flour
1/4 Teaspoon Salt
1 Cup Butter
1/2 Cup Sugar
Powdered Sugar

Combine first 6 ingredients and form 1-inch balls. Bake on cookie sheet 1-inch apart. After baked, put about 5 cookies at a time in plastic bag with powdered sugar and shake gently to coat. Put on rack and continue with the remainder of cookies. You may want to double this recipe, because they disappear fast.

Pignoli Cookies (Pine Nut Cookies)

These are very delicious Sicilian cookies. The Sicilians are known for their pastries. These were one of the cookies they made for weddings. Excellent.

Yield: 36 Servings

1/2 Pound Almond Paste
1/2 Cup Very Fine Sugar
1/2 Teaspoon Baking Powder
1/4 Cup Egg Whites
1 Cup Pine Nuts

In a mixing bowl mix almond paste and sugar and baking powder. Add egg whites and mix well. Put pine nuts in small bowl. With a teaspoon take some dough the size of a walnut, drop it in the pine nuts and press dough into pine nuts and lay each on cookie sheet lined with parchment paper. Bake at 350 degrees for 15 to 20 minutes till they are golden. Let cookies cool on sheet for 5 minutes, transfer to racks, let cool completely. Store cookies in tight container.

Note: A pastry bag with wide nozzle may be used to drop dough into pine nuts.

Sesame Seed Cookies

Another Sicilian cookie. This one melts in your mouth, although crunchy. This is very well liked. You can't stop at one.

Yield: 48 Servings

1 Cup Sugar
1 1/2 Cup Vegetable Shortening
3 Large Eggs
1 Teaspoon Vanilla
2 1/2 Cups Unbleached Flour
1 Cup Cornstarch
1 Teaspoon Baking Powder
1/2 Teaspoon Salt
1/2 Pound Sesame Seeds
Milk for coating

Cream the sugar and shortening. Beat the eggs and vanilla, mix them well into the shortening and sugar. Sift together the flour, cornstarch, baking powder and salt two times. Add slowly to the wet ingredients until it is all absorbed. The result should be a soft dough. If it is too sticky, add more flour, too dry, add some milk. Form the dough into a ball, flour it and cover it with a cloth, let rest in refrigerator for half hour. Take a piece of the dough and using your hands, roll it the thickness of your finger or 3/4 inch thick, using flour if necessary. Cut 3-inch lengths. Coat each piece with milk and roll in sesame seeds. Continue with the rest of the dough. Place on a greased cookie sheet an inch apart. Bake in center of the oven, preheated 375 degrees, until they golden brown, about 20 to 25 minutes.

Thumbprint Cookies

Thumbprint Cookies are very popular, especially around Christmas.

Yield: 40

1 Cup Butter or Margarine
2/3 Cup Sugar
2 Egg Yolks
1/2 Teaspoon Vanilla
2 1/4 Cups All Purpose Flour
1/4 Teaspoon Salt

Cream butter; gradually add sugar, beating on medium speed of an electric mixer until light and fluffy. Add egg yolks one at a time, beating well after each addition. Stir in vanilla. Combine flour and salt; add to cream mixture, mixing well. Chill dough at least 1 hour. Shape dough into 1-inch balls; place about 2 inches apart on ungreased cookie sheets Press thumb in each cookie leaving an indention. Bake at 300 degrees for 20 to 25 minutes, do not brown. Cool on wire racks. Spoon about 1/2 teaspoon of fruit preserves of your choice into the thumb depression. Or try this chocolate frosting: Combine 1 cup sugar, 1/4 cup cocoa, 1/4 cup milk, 1/4 cup butter or margarine, and 1/2 teaspoon vanilla.

Apple Danish

This a simple dessert to make and it is very well liked. (Dad's sister) Aunt Lily used to make something like this. She added cornflakes in her pastry.

Yield: 20 Servings

3 Cups Flour
1/2 Teaspoon Salt
1 Cup Shortening
1 Egg Yolk
1/2 Cup Milk
Filling:
3 Apples, Peeled, Sliced
1 1/2 Cups Sugar
1/4 Cup Butter, Melted
2 Tablespoons Flour
1 Teaspoon Cinnamon
1 Egg White, Lightly Beaten
Glaze:
1/2 Cup Confectioners Sugar
2 to 3 Teaspoons Water

In a mixing bowl, combine flour and salt; cut in shortening until mixture resembles coarse crumbs. Combine egg yolk and milk; add to flour mixture. Stir just until dough clings together. Divide dough in half. On a lightly floured surface, roll half the dough into a 15 X 1-inch X 1 inch baking pan. Set aside. In a bowl toss together filling ingredients; spoon over pastry in pan. Roll out remaining dough to another 15 inch X 10 inch rectangle. Place over filling. Brush with egg white. Bake at 375 degree for 40 minutes or until golden brown. Cool on a wire rack. Combine the confectioners sugar and enough water to achieve a drizzling consistency. Drizzle over warm pastry. Cut into squares.

Coconut Custard Pie

You can use all cream instead of milk if you like a richer custard and add a little more coconut.

Yield: 12 Servings

1 1/2 Cups Milk
1 1/2 Cups Half & Half
1/2 Cup Sugar
1/8 Teaspoon Salt
6 Eggs, Slightly Beaten
1 Teaspoon Vanilla
12-Inch Pie Crust
1/2 Cup Sweetened Coconut

Scald milk, Half & Half, and sugar, and salt in a double boiler, remove from the fire and add slowly to the slightly beaten eggs and vanilla, and mix well. Add coconut to custard. Pour into deep-dish baked pie crust, and be careful not to fill it too full. Bake in moderate oven 350 degrees for about 25 minutes, or until the custard is set in the center.

Cranberry Relish

This recipe was one of (my daughter-in-law's mother) Mrs. Taylor's favorite. She would always make this for Thanksgiving. Everyone liked it. Now we still make it for Thanksgiving dinner.

Yield: 15 Servings

2 Packages Cherry Gelatin
1 Cup Sugar
2 Cups Hot Water
1 Orange
1 Apple
1 Stalk Celery, Chopped
1 Pound Raw Cranberries

Mix cherry gelatin and sugar in hot water. Grind cranberries, apple, orange, and celery. Stir into gelatin. Mix well and put in refrigerator until gelatin is set.

French Cream Icing

Note from us kids: This is the icing Mom used for years on her famous multi-tiered wedding cakes and birthday cakes that she made and decorated for us. We loved it.

Yield: 10 servings (enough for a medium-size cake)

1 Cup Milk
3/4 Cup Presto Flour
1/4 Cup Margarine
1/4 Cup Sweet Butter
1/2 Cup Crisco
3/4 Cup Sugar (granulated)
1 Teaspoon Vanilla

Place milk and flour in double boiler or cook over low flame. Cook until the roux is the consistency of thick mashed potatoes, stirring all the time. Place in a small bowl. Cover with plastic wrap and cool. In mixing bowl place margarine, butter, and Crisco. Blend well. Add sugar and vanilla and blend. Then add milk-flour roux. Beat 10-12 minutes on medium speed.

Variations:
Mocha Icing: Add 4 tablespoons cocoa to sugar and follow above procedure.
Marshmallow Icing: Use 1 cup Crisco (instead of 1/2) omitting margarine and butter. Follow same procedure, beating mixture 15 minutes high speed.
Fruit flavored icing: After all the blending is done, add some strained crushed pineapples, peaches, strawberries of any fruit you desire and blend by hand.

I Remember Mama

Tom (son): In early 1978, my wife, Patty, and I bought a manual pasta making machine at a small (restaurant supply) store on Hanover Street in Boston's North End neighborhood. We paid about $35 for the machine and thought that was quite expensive but Mom had recommended the brand and model. The only place we could find it was in a supply store that was not far from where we lived. Today, you can go on-line to Amazon and find a similar make/model (restaurant grade) for about $500.

We still have the original machine and continue to use it quite often throughout the year. In fact, many of you have had several occasions to try the final product that this machine produces under Patty's skillful hand. My daughters, Carmela and Christina, have similar but less expensive models and often use their machines, having learned the "trade" from their Mom—and to some degree their Dad :>).

My oldest, Carmela, often makes the pasta, usually ravioli, with Isabella, her young daughter. Isabella has become quite proficient at handling the pasta and really enjoys the "chore" when they make the ravioli, such as they did recently. Of course, it was for their family celebration of the Thanksgiving holiday. Yes, they continue the Sicilian tradition of serving ravioli first and later the turkey and trimmings. Isabella loves it so much that she asked her Mom if they could have a "ravioli making party" with some of her friends. She wants to invite them all to their home and show them how to make ravioli since none of them has heard of such a thing, much less had the opportunity to make pasta. However, they all know they love ravioli. It's too bad Mom didn't get a chance to find out about the planned "ravioli making party." However, Mom's passion and expertise in cooking live on. She has inspired so far at least three generations of "chefs" with a real promise to continue long into the future.

*Mom & Dad 50 years together
and many more to come, 1991.*

*Dad: "Sicilians are sensational."
Don't argue.*

Sfinci 'i San Giuseppi (Puffs For St Joseph)

This is a treat that is usually made for the feast of Saint Joseph, which is celebrated March 19. They are almost like cream puffs, but they are deep fried and they can be filled with custard or eaten plain. We eat them so fast, there isn't time for custard. Delicious

Yield: 24 Servings

1 Cup Unsalted Butter
2 Cups Water
2 Cups Unbleached Flour, Sifted
8 Large Eggs
3/4 Cup Honey
1/4 Cup Water
1/2 Teaspoon Cinnamon
2 Quarts Light Oil, Canola
Powdered Sugar

Melt the butter in 2 cups water in a saucepan. When it comes to a boil, stir in the sifted flour. Remove from heat and turn into a bowl. Add the eggs one at a time, mixing thoroughly before adding another. Let the batter cool. Meanwhile, place the honey, 1/4 cup water, and cinnamon in a small saucepan on the stove, but do not heat it yet. Pour the oil in 3 1/2-quart pot and heat it until 375 degrees. When the oil is ready, take a mounded soup spoon of the batter, and using a second soup spoon, scrape it off and drop it into the oil. Fry until golden brown and hollow inside and then remove from the oil with a slotted spoon. Place on brown paper to absorb the excess grease. Place *sfinci* on a warmed serving platter. When the *sfinci* (doughnuts) are nearly all cooked heat the honey and cinnamon. When the liquid comes to a boil, turn down the heat and keep it warm until all of the *sfinci* are cooked and arranged on the platter. Pour the honey over them, dust with powdered sugar and serve immediately. I have done these without using the honey. I just dust the doughnuts with powdered sugar. You may want to try either way.

I Remember Mama

Chuck (son): I was just seven. We were still living in Elizabeth where the first four of us kids went to Blessed Sacrament grammar school. I was about to make my First Holy Communion there. The night before Mom had made the cream puffs, which she planned to fill the next day with the custard, something she only made on special occasions. The morning of my First Communion I saw the platter of cream puffs. Next to Mom's coconut custard pie, I loved her cream puffs best, so I snitched one and started to appease my hunger. Mom saw me and grabbed me and started emptying my mouth of the food. In those days you had to fast from midnight—you could drink water but no food. She made sure I hadn't swallowed any. But I sure indulged later when there was company and I could savor more than one cream puff.

Apple Crisp

I found this recipe at the hospital, put there by a dietitian. It's simple and easy on the calories. I made this and it was a hit.

Yield: 8 Servings

Vegetable Oil Spray
1 1/2 Pounds (5 Medium Apples), Cored and Sliced
2 Tablespoons Fresh Lemon Juice
1/4 Teaspoon Ground Cinnamon
2/3 Cup All-Purpose Flour
1/2 Cup Firmly Packed Brown Sugar
1/2 Cup Uncooked Oatmeal
1/3 Cup Margarine or Butter

Preheat oven to 375 degrees. Lightly spray a 2-quart casserole dish with vegetable oil spray. Arrange apples in prepared dish. Sprinkle with lemon juice and cinnamon. In medium bowl, combine flour, brown sugar and oatmeal. Cut in margarine with a fork or pastry blender until mixture is crumbly. Spread over fruit. Bake 40 minutes or until apples are tender.

Almond Pear Pie

I made this pie and it made a big hit and it is delicious.

Yield: 8 Servings

Pastry For One 9-Inch Pie Shell
Custard Filling
1/4 Cup Plus 2 Tablespoons Sugar
1/4 Teaspoon Salt
1 1/2 Tablespoons Cornstarch
1 1/2 Cups Milk
3 Egg Yolks, Slightly Beaten
3/4 Teaspoon Vanilla Extract
1/4 Teaspoon Almond Extract
1/4 Cup Almond Paste
1 Can Pear Halves (1 Pound 14 Oz.), Well Drained
1/2 Cup Apricot Preserves, Melted
1/2 Cup Heavy Cream
2 Tablespoons Confectionery Sugar

Preheat oven to 450 degrees. On very lightly floured pastry cloth, with a stockinette-covered rolling pin, roll pastry with light strokes from center to edge to an 11-inch circle. Trim to make even edge. Fold in half. With fold in center, place in a 9-inch pie plate. Unfold pastry and fit into pie plate, pressing toward center to eliminate air bubbles under crust and to reduce shrinkage. Fold under edge of crust, press into an upright rim. Crimp edge decoratively. Prick surface evenly with fork. Refrigerate about 1/2 hour. Bake shell 8 minutes or until golden-brown. Cool on rack.

Make *filling*: In small saucepan, mix granulated sugar, salt, and cornstarch with wooden spoon. Stir in milk. Cook, stirring, over medium heat until mixture thickens and thickens and begins to boil; boil 1 minute. Stir a little hot mixture into egg yolks; pour back into saucepan. Stir in vanilla and almond extracts. Cook, stirring constantly until mixture is thick. Pour into medium bowl; place waxed paper directly on surface. Refrigerate for 1 hour. *(continued)*

To assemble: Roll almond paste between two sheets of waxed paper into 6-inch circle. Remove top sheet. Invert paste on bottom of pie shell; remove paper and spread paste with custard. Arrange drained pears around edge. Brush with melted preserves. In small bowl, beat heavy cream with confectioner's' sugar until stiff. Fill pastry bag with number 6 star tip with whipped cream; pipe swirls between pear halves and in center of pie. Refrigerate 2 hours. To serve cut pie into wedges.

Apple Pie

Apple pie is an all-American dessert. There are many different ways this pie has been made, but I stick to the simple way it was done before recipe books.

Yield: 12 Servings

5 or 6 Large Apples, Delicious or Green Apples
1/2 Cup Sugar
1 Teaspoon Cinnamon
1 Large Tablespoon Flour or Cornstarch
2 12-inch Unbaked Pastries (top and bottom)
1 Egg Beaten To Paint Top of Pastry

Peel and slice apples in a bowl. Add sugar and cinnamon and mix well. Add flour or cornstarch and mix. Line pie plate with pastry. Add apples, cover top of apples add the top pastry. Beat one egg and paint top of pastry. Bake 400 degrees for 15 minutes then lower temperature to 350 degrees. Bake till top is nice and brown about 40 minutes.

Pineapple Pie
I got this recipe from my friend Ninette. She only shares this with certain people.

Yield: 6 Servings

30 ounces Crushed Pineapple, Drained, Save Juice
1 Cup Sugar
5 Tablespoons Cornstarch
One 10-Inch Pie Crust

Preheat oven to 350 F.
Heat pineapple juice with sugar and cornstarch in sauce pot on medium heat, or in a double boiler. Heat just to boil. Mix in crushed pineapple and pour into pie shell. Bake for 20 minutes with foil around crust to keep it from burning. Remove foil and bake 20 minutes more. Delicious.

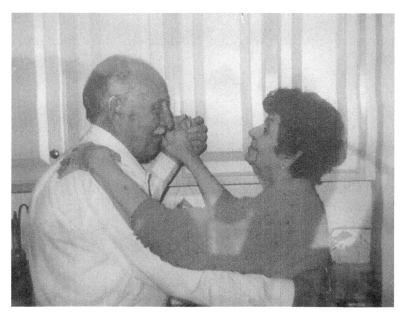

Always time to dance.

Baklava

This is a Greek dessert. It is very rich, but delicious. Easy but it takes a little time.

Yield: 20 Servings

Pastry:
1 Pound Walnuts
1/2 Cup Sugar
2 Teaspoons Cinnamon
1 Pound Butter, Melted
1 Pound Filo dough
Syrup:
1 1/2 Cups of Water
3 Cups Sugar
1 Cup Honey
Juice of 1/2 Lemon

Pastry: Combine coarsely ground walnuts with sugar and cinnamon. Set aside. Line bottom of buttered pan, 9 X 12-inches, with filo, brushing each sheet with melted butter. Sprinkle next sheet with nuts. Cover with another 3 sheets of filo, brushing melted butter on each sheet. Sprinkle with more nut mixture. Repeat process, until all nut mixture is used. Cover with remaining buttered filo. Chill 25 minutes. *Make the syrup:* Combine water, sugar, and honey. Boil 10 minutes. Add lemon juice and simmer 5 minutes longer.

Cut the chilled pastry into small diamond shapes. Bake in a slow oven 325 degrees for 1 to 1/2 hours. When slightly brown, remove from oven. Slowly pour enough cooled syrup over hot baklava until completely absorbed.

Note: Baklava should be hot and syrup cold, or vice versa. When cooled cover with foil, never with plastic wrap because this tends to soften crust.

Key Lime Pie

I found this recipe in Cooks Magazine. I liked this recipe for the summer—no baking.

Yield: 12 Servings

Crust:
8 Whole Graham Crackers Broken In Pieces
2 Tablespoons Sugar
5 Tablespoons Unsalted Butter, Melted
Filling
1/4 Cup Sugar
1 Tablespoon Grated Lime Zest
8 Ounces Cream Cheese
1 (14-Ounce) Sweetened Condensed Milk
1/3 Cup Instant Vanilla Pudding
1 1/4 Teaspoons Unflavored Gelatin
1 Cup Fresh Lime Juice, 6 To 8 Limes
1 Teaspoon Vanilla

Crust: Grind crackers and combine with add sugar and melted butter. Press crumbs firmly into bottom and sides of 9-inch pie plate. Bake until fragrant and browned around the edges, 12 to 14 minutes. Cool completely.

Filling: Process sugar and zest in food processor until sugar turns bright green, about 30 seconds. Add cream cheese and process until combined, about 30 seconds. Add condensed milk and pudding mix and process until smooth, about 30 seconds Scrape down sides of bowl. Stir gelatin and 2 tablespoons lime juice in small bowl. Heat in microwave for 15 seconds; stir until dissolved. With machine running pour gelatin mixture, remaining lime juice and vanilla through feed tube and mix until thoroughly combined, about 30 seconds. Pour into cooled pie shell. Refrigerate till set about 8 hours.

Everybody, Sing Along!

Ohhh, we are the Cusumanos,

you've heard so much about

People stop and stare at us whenever we go out

We noted for our winning ways

In everything we do

Everybody likes us

We hope you like us too . . .

Mom & Dad's 50th Anniversary, July, 1991

Books by Carmela Cusumano's Children and Grandchildren

James A. Cusumano:
Life is Beautiful, 12 Universal Rules, (Waterfront Press-2016) ISBN 978-1-943625-19-2 (print)
ISBN-978-1-943625-18-5 (e-book)
Balance: The Business-Life Connection, (SelectBooks-2013) ISBN 13: 978-159079-960-4 (print)
ISBN 10 1590799607 (e-book)
Cosmic Consciousness, A Journey to Well-being, Happiness and Success (Fortuna Libri-), Kindle Edition, ASIN B0058EWT5M
Freedom From Mid-East Oil, (World Business Academy Press-2007) ISBN 978-0979405-22-8

Salvatore J. Cusumano:
Introduction to Laser Weapon Systems Glen P. Perram, Salvatore J. Cusumano, Robert L. Hengehold, and Steven T. Fiorino; Directed Energy Professional Society, 7770 Jefferson Street NE, Suite 440, Albuquerque, New Mexico 87109
ISBN-13 978-0-9793687-4-5

John Hennessy:
Coney Island Pilgrims, poetry ISBN-13: 978-0912592985
Bridge & Tunnel, poetry, ISBN 1933456558

Sabina Murray (all fiction):
Forgery, ISBN: 10: 0802143687
The Caprices, ISBN-10: 080214313X
ISBN-13: 978-0802143136
A Carnivore's Inquiry, ISBN: 0802142001
Tales of the New World, ISBN-10: 0802170838
ISBN-13: 978-0802170835
Slow Burn, ISBN-10: 0345367731
ISBN-13: 978-0345367730

Camille Cusumano:
The Last Cannoli (Legas), A novel about a Sicilian American family

caught between the glories of the old country and the promise of prosperity in America ISBN-10: 1881901203
ISBN-13: 978-1881901204

Tango, an Argentine Love Story (Seal Press) ISBN-10:1580052509

*Italy, A Love Story (*Seal Press), ISBN-10: 158005143X
ISBN-13: 978-1580051439

France, A Love Story (Seal Press) ISBN-10: 0760791309
ISBN-13: 978-0760791301

Tango Fantasia, A Tango Lover's Collection of Three Tango Books (Centanni) ISBN: 978-0997049824

Coming in 2016 by Camille Cusumano (memoir):

Wilderness Begins at Home
Travels With My Big Sicilian Family
Centanni Publications,
ISBN-13: 978-0997049831
ISBN-10: 0997049839

243
250
255
270
288

Made in the USA
Middletown, DE
03 March 2021